Who Owns
the Problem?

Who Owns the Problem?

AFRICA AND THE STRUGGLE FOR AGENCY

Pius Adesanmi

Michigan State University | East Lansing

Michigan State University Press
East Lansing, Michigan 48823-5245

Printed and bound in the United States of America.

29   28   27   26   25   24   23   22   21   20   1   2   3   4   5   6   7   8   9   10

LIBRARY OF CONGRESS CATALOGING-IN-PUBLICATION DATA

Names: Adesanmi, Pius, author. | Falola, Toyin, writer of foreword. | Harrow, Kenneth W., writer of foreword.
Title: Who owns the problem? : Africa and the struggle for agency / Pius Adesanmi.
Other titles: African humanities and the arts.
Description: East Lansing : Michigan State University Press, 2020.
| Series: African humanities and the arts | Includes bibliographical references and index.
| Identifiers: LCCN 2019028371 | ISBN 978-1-61186-355-0 (paperback)
| ISBN 978-1-60917-630-3 | ISBN 978-1-62895-392-3 | ISBN 978-1-62896-393-9
Subjects: LCSH: Literature and society—Africa. | Literature and society—Nigeria.
| Africa—Social conditions—21st century. | Nigeria—Social conditions—21st century.
| Africa—Intellectual life—21st century. | Nigeria—Intellectual life—21st century.
Classification: LCC DT14 .A3 2020 | DDC 960.33--dc23
LC record available at https://lccn.loc.gov/2019028371

Book design and typesetting by Charlie Sharp, Sharp Designs, East Lansing, Michigan
Cover design by Erin Kirk New
Cover art is *Lagos Afternoon* by Victor Ehikhamenor @victorsozaboy

Michigan State University Press is a member of the Green Press Initiative and is committed to developing
and encouraging ecologically responsible publishing practices. For more information about the Green
Press Initiative and the use of recycled paper in book publishing, please visit www.greenpressinitiative.org.

Visit Michigan State University Press at *www.msupress.org*

Contents

More Than Just a Name

Toyin Falola

Writing this piece is difficult for me. It brings me closer to the reality of Pius Adesanmi's passing, which I am still struggling to come to terms with. Death, of course, is a welcome phenomenon in the Yoruba worldview that I and several other friends and colleagues share with Adesanmi. Although we would wish that a person dies at a considerably old age, we still realize the fact that one could die at an early age. We know well, as the saying goes, that *Ogún ọmọdé ò lè ṣeré fún ogún odún* ("twenty young children cannot play together for twenty years"). Among other factors, death will definitely break this circle and its union. Despite this realization, the death of a young person will still always be a great shock to us, especially if the person is the kind one would describe as *ọmọ àtàtà* (a beloved child), *ọmọ ológo* (a child of glory), and *ọmọlúàbí* (a person of virtue). Pius epitomized such characteristics, and this is why the news of his death put the world into a fit of grief. The sting of death that cut Pius in his prime creates inconsolable sorrow. *Ikú d'óró—ikú ṣèkà.* An irreplaceable man has gone. The sorrow is difficult to bear. The pain refuses to leave.

A branch has fallen
Stricken down by Ṣàngó

The god of thunder
Stolen by death
To appease Ògún, the god of iron

Is this a sacrifice?
Why not collect a chicken?
Yes, death collected a chicken by violence
A hawk that sweeps the chicken off the ground
The mother hen is powerless

Òrúnmìlà, why do you look away?
No emissary to the forest
To prevent the ìrókò from falling
Killing the tallest tree in the jungle
A sting of death that refuses appeasement

Ṣokotí, Alágbẹ̀dẹ Ọ̀run
Ṣokotí forged and pounded metal, to create and destroy

The beloved and glorious person that Pius was is not only evident in the fact that he was able to lay a professional path for himself, but to connect his work with the aspirations of millions of young people who see a different world. This is just a dream, a goal, what everybody lives for. Beyond this, Pius had a passion, what he looked up to—not everybody has this. And this was to be a tremendous and positive influence for Africa and the rest of the world. He was not just a university professor; he was both gown and town. Pius's students and protégés are not only those he would have conversations with in the four walls of the classroom or meet with during office hours. Many more are on Facebook and Twitter as his friends and followers. This *ọmọlúàbí* practically turned social media into a classroom. All the high sublimity and carefully chosen diction of his writings clearly bear messages for people, even for the human population in the remotest corners of the world. He qualified for the title *olùkọ́ni rere*—a humane teacher—a term first used by Nicodemus for Jesus Christ and later deployed for pioneer missionary educators whom the Yoruba deemed to be selfless and worthy.

Until his sudden and unfortunate death—I can't believe this reality is dawning on me—Pius was on the path to becoming a major public intellectual like Ali

Mazrui, making sociocultural contributions for mainstream audiences, all in an effort to transform Africa. Pius had both human and intellectual high qualities in abundance. He sought coherence and wholeness in both theory and practice. His methodology did not see society as a silo, understandable as autonomous and without context. He was a conscientious, meticulous scholar who graced his craft with wit, integrity, dedication, and enthusiasm. His energy and enthusiasm for everything that life had to offer was infectious and inspiring. People who knew him would admire his strength, his passion, his resilience, his exuberance, and his adorably audacious character. I happen to be one of those people. *T'ọmọ ẹni bá dára, ọ yẹ ká wi.* Pius was a gem, a wit; *gbogbo ara kìkì ọgbọ́n bí Ifá.*

Those in the literary world are usually not found in the policy world, but Pius was good in literature and politics, art and economics. Operating with a rare and unequalled rapidity, Pius spent his life between academic rituals and practical engagements, shaping the minds of thousands of young Africans, preparing them for the purpose of revolutionizing and reforming the continent. He was enjoining and challenging them to see themselves as the core of the national project and to stand up for their rights. In the same vein, he was commanding the attention of intelligentsias, corporate bodies, social and political circles, and other forums and institutions in Africa, North America, and Europe. He demonstrated to them what Africa is and what it is not, allowing them see the best way to relate to Africa as a continent of humans and as a sociocultural entity. Yet in all this he was a centrist. He knew the Yoruba moral philosophy of *tùbûnùbí* (amicable settlement), and he applied it. He would scold Africans where necessary and would clearly point out to the world's economic and political superpowers where they had wronged Africa and the need to make amends.

Very rapidly, his influence spread across the continent, as he spoke about the power of knowledge, spreading words of comfort, addressing issues around the relevance of resistance to power. He opened the way to a larger discourse on the limits of superstructures, while also creating a path to extensive reflections on the social and cultural formations of contemporary Africa. Focusing on quotidian lived experiences, he connected thousands of people with the bigger ambition of the application of an Africa-centered modernity. Pius understood the core of the capitalist system, set against the context of the rural background of his parentage. He became audacious, seeking for ways to transform the rural into the modern, and the means to tame capitalism into a system with a soul. He stayed in the heart of capitalism but with his mind in the rural where his heart was. He successfully created a community using language to capture the minds of his constituencies. His *Ujamah* became eager listeners, and they began to share a common understanding about the future of Africa. As his reputation became established, he also became a catalyst and innovator, driving ideas around the empowerment of youth to create emancipation movements, resistance tools, and national liberation. He mastered the art of combining theory with practice, political criticisms with theoretical debates, militant passion with sound intellectual data.

Indeed, Pius had set the pace for the transformation of Africa in the twenty-first century. This posthumous publication, *Who Owns the Problem: Africa and the Struggle for Agency,* is unarguably a masterpiece in this regard. It is clearly representative of the unique intellectual prowess and creative valor that was Pius Adesanmi's. All the essays in this book are neither simple nor complex; they are the best of both. They are written in a grand style and elevated structure, yet they constitute a book as much for the public as it is for the academic community and the world of letters. The book commands the close interaction and critical attention of the reader, with nothing obscure or abstract about the thematic thrust of the book. Each word in the book carries propelling meaning; each sentence is colorfully thought-provoking.

In this book, Pius unequivocally demonstrates the need for African agency in order to transform the continent. He enjoins Africans to be the agents that will identify, define, and narrate African problems and also report the continent's progress. This role of agency, he points out, is currently being played by outsiders—individuals and institutions alike—and this is why the continent still remains stuck in negative stereotypes and pushed to the beggar's floor. To lift Africa up from its subaltern state, Pius exhorts the people of Africa to be the pivotal agents. Pointing out the interconnections between culture and civilization, Adesanmi shows that the modernity which Africans and African nation-states now seek cannot be achieved outside African value systems. Therefore, he calls for Africans to stop discouraging and stigmatizing African cultural practices, products, and perspectives if truly they desire genuine growth, development, and progress in the continent.

With my generation of Africanist scholars getting closer to the exit point, I personally took Pius to be at the vanguard of the new generation. I was sure the baton was in the right hands. My hope was brightened. But then the hope was dashed and crashed with Ethiopian Airlines Flight 302. Now a great fear has descended upon me. I am afraid that his sudden and unfortunate death might create a big, deep, and dark gap between the present and the future of Africa. This fear can only be averted if African scholars at home and in the Diaspora are ready to take up the task of enlivening and giving meanings to, in theory and practice, the Africanist passion that Pius embodied through his professorial position, writings, speeches, and general lifestyle. His students and protégés in the academic community and his foot soldiers on social media must also continue to honor and respect his distinguished memory.

Pius was more than just a name. Like the sun, like the moon, he was an impactful presence exuding life, vitality, hope, and positivity. Pius lived up to the Murid ethos that the great African Sufi leader Ahmadu Bamba taught to all of us: seek excellence in whatever you do and be a blessing to humans to serve God. He was a prophet, and his teachings must not be forgotten. Rather, his number of apostles must continue to increase by the day. He was a spirit of revolution and positive reform. He must live on through the effort of every individual to seek progress for Africa. This is the only way we can fight back against death, the great trickster that robbed us of Pius in broad daylight.

Foreword

Kenneth W. Harrow

Pius Adesanmi became the voice for his generation, before the Ethiopian Airlines crash of March 10, 2019, took his life. His work as a graduate student bridged Francophone and Anglophone Africa. He quickly moved, after graduating from the University of British Columbia in 2002, to an important assistant professorship at Penn State and, shortly thereafter, to Carleton University in Ottawa where he directed the university's Institute of African Studies as well as teaching African studies. His voice, often satiric, and his highly informed plumbing of issues of greatest import to today's Africa could be encountered frequently in his columns for Sahara Reporters. But more significantly, he published a collection of essays in *You're not a Country, Africa* (2011) that won the inaugural Penguin Prize for African Writing in the nonfiction category. He had marked out a path that was to lead him to great success, one defined by the essay that would enable him to express his thoughts before live audiences as well as publish online columns and on Facebook to thousands of followers. He was, almost immediately, the public intellectual who had become indispensable. The airline crash stole our ebullient, insightful, young colleague, leaving us to limp behind him.

In Yoruba thought, Eshu, a little impish deity in disguise, limped. Pius granted us this limp, not because we would have chosen to have it—who wants to struggle to walk—but because he had fashioned the style that corresponded to our times. To find out what the issues were that preoccupied him, it will be necessary to read this book, his last volume, that was in production as the accident occurred. Too much pain will come from reflecting on that crash; our compensation for the loss will have to be the reconstruction of his voice as he delivers these speeches to us, one after another. I wrote the introduction that follows before I had received the bad news. I insist that we now return to the memory of this friend in order to celebrate his work and his warmth and humor.

In *Who Owns the Problem?*, Pius Adesanmi offers the reader a collection of his remarkable keynote addresses given over the better part of the second decade of the twenty-first century. He speaks to a broad range of topics, generally speaking from the podium, to African, Canadian, and American audiences—including academics and business and government people—the informed and educated with an abiding interest in African affairs and letters. One is struck from the outset with his assumption that his listeners have a broad and deep literacy, a knowledge of African authors, politics, social, cultural, and economic affairs, so as to respond to his evocation of weighty current topics. If for nothing else, this collection of commentaries opens the reader to a compelling vision of contemporary Africa, inviting engagement in terms of today's radical changes from the past. Radical in the way that a palm-wine tapper is imagined to be calling his sleepy customer early in the morning, to inform him that some nasty thieves had already preceded him up the tree and tapped out his favorite brew. That customer was Adesanmi himself, who cannot help but imagine what it might mean for his father's tapper to be up there taking selfies while passing on the bad news to our speaker.

But what I wish to signal in this preface is not so much the range of topics, the originality of the voice that addresses us with wit, charm, and vitality, but more importantly the genre of writing that is employed. It is very rare to find in Africanist writings a collection of essays that is not narrowly scholarly, or that doesn't offer popularizing accounts of "Africa" as exemplifying problems of conflict, poverty, resource expropriation, etc.—that is, variants of journalistic writing. Adesanmi's essays are beautifully constructed reflections on issues of key importance to the literary scholar, which he himself also happens to be, and to the audience familiar with these issues. He centers the locus of his reflections around his own circumstances, that of a Nigerian—specifically Yoruba—author, who grew up as part of what he calls the third generation of authors, and yet who has been traveling across the African continent and across North America, particularly Canada, where he teaches, and the United States. More pertinently, he centers his reflections around one particular concern that drives the arguments repeatedly, albeit from multiple directions, and that is a form of love for Nigeria, in particular, and generally African culture, that demands that he express the values that have emerged from the work of Africans.

■ ■ ■

In his talk on feminism he contests the limited Eurocentric understanding of feminist theory that encompasses only French feminism and its heirs in the 1980s and 1990s in the United States, without taking into account the rising accomplishments of African women writers, like Obioma Nnaemeka, Catherine Ocholonu, and Molara Ogundipe-Leslie, who have aimed to ground their understandings of gender issues in African social worlds. If it is the developments in world cinema, he will remind the reader of the effulgent growth of Nollywood and its offshoots. If it is technological innovations, he will expand upon the widespread embrace of social media, and its stars, including Ikhide and others who have chosen Facebook, Twitter, and the like. If it is Western feminism that has generated its canon of theorists, beginning with the Irigarays and Kristevas, Spivaks and Butlers—that is, poststructuralist or Lacanian psychoanalytical figures—his reproach will be, when standing on African soil, when its standpoint epistemology is located in Lagos rather than Paris or New York, well, doesn't an African woman also count? Aint I a theorist, too, or is the field limited to only the owners of the Western word:

> I am used to the West constantly proclaiming the originality of some new proposition in the arena of knowledge largely because Western canonizers of knowledge are very much like the child in that Yoruba proverb who, never having visited other people's farms, screams from the rooftop that his father owns the biggest farm in the world.

If the issues are compelling, the writing is where Adesanmi is truly original. The tone is enduringly appealing, highly personal, educated, and challenging. He often takes a tiny thread and spins and spins it into major reflections that address through the African optic the key moments of our times. In one essay he takes on Paul Zeleza's push to counter Afro-pessimist language over issues like Ebola and, in placing his biography in the position of a central coordinate, identifies the cultural shift that would mark the response to the negativity:

My generation came of age in the 1980s, writing tests and exams on foolscap sheets. Jacques de Larosiere and his successor at the IMF, Michel Camdessus, sealed our fate with policies rammed down the throat of one military dictator after another across the continent. Today, the youth who make Africa tick are on Facebook and Twitter grumbling about the size of iPhone 6 even as Christine Lagarde declares enthusiastically that an appropriate "policy mix" will be worked out to ensure a "good bailout" for Ghana. I am of the '70s/'80s. A generation came of age in the '90s. Another came of age in the 2000s. Three generations of Africans, only one uniting factor: Bretton Woods's policy "mixes." With Christine Lagarde talking about Ghana in 2014 like Getafix the Druid in the *Asterix* comic series, a speaker not as optimistic as my humble self would say that we have come full circle in Africa.

Having placed his generation midway between that of the "fathers," including Soyinka, Achebe, Clark, and Okigbo, and their great-grandchildren, whose names he multiplies vertiginously, he situates the argument between Afro-pessimism and Afro-optimism in the moment defined by more than youths' iPhones:

> However, beyond this happy marriage of logic and political correctness lies nuance. If we agree that elation and celebration have as much *droit de cité* in the African story as depression, gloom, and doom, we must ask the questions: how exactly did elation come into this picture? What is its trajectory? What are its contents? How do we account for the politics of back and forth between depression and elation and what does it portend for disciplinary engagements of Africa?

The phrasings around "elation" point to more than the intellectual counter to the negativities associated with past attempts to counter bleak prognostications about the continent and its people. It marks his determination to make an African voice be heard, and to adopt the stage of the public intellectual in the service of that cause. The trajectory of "elation" is set in place by the very language that poses the problem of its presence, already elaborated in great detail across the disciplines that include the musical, plastic, culinary, fashion, and literary arts that he will evoke again in highly personal terms: the dances he and his costudents performed in Vancouver when a student; the tasty dishes his friends prepared and consumed; the club they frequented... the elation of sharing a world of West African pleasures and locutions.

Where does an African agency come into question, when so many "experts" like Lagarde prescribe the terms for an "Africa Rising"? It comes in the language of the public essay that takes its place in the forum, spoken in response to the call of the public conference of those who expect the language marked by palm oil and applaud the eneke bird's sentiments:

> Africa Rising invites us to take a closer look at the question of African agency. As one looks at the glass display cases of triumphalist and exultant neoliberalism, many African countries are on display: Ghana, Botswana, South Africa, Kenya, Namibia, etc. After every election meeting the minimal requirements of democracy, new countries are installed in new glass display cases and brandished to the world as the latest success stories from Africa. Yet, as you window-shop and look at these African countries glistening in display cases, your mind returns again and again to the question of agency. What was the African's role in the construction of these glass showcases, and what say did he have in the politics of inhabiting that glass display case?

We need look no further than here to find an answer to the question of where the metaphor of this glass showcase appeared so as to enable us to affirm the presence of an African agency—an agency, grounded in the clear-eyed insistence of Adesanmi, to construct in these essays a plethora of glass displays. Within the cases might appear the display of stylish clothing, like a woman's headcloth, or the cityscapes overrun by NGO presences, made visible in their jeeps. Whirlwind displays, where we can look and laugh, even so as to cover the sad reality behind the jokiness of the language in describing Accra's "postcolonial jeepiness":

> It was the jeeps! There were way too many jeeps on the roads of Accra for my liking. No, I am not talking about private jeeps belonging to individuals. I am talking about what I call postcolonial jeepology, a phenomenon in which jeeps bring the symbolism of foreign aid and dependency to the doorsteps of the postcolony. You should be able to visualize those UN jeeps by now. I mean those white Toyota Prado jeeps that are so ubiquitous in Africa. They bear the insignia of every imaginable specialized agency of the United Nations: FAO, UNICEF, UNCHS, WHO, etc. The glut of white jeeps.

In the end, it is not so much the remarks about the ubiquitous presence of NGOs that strike us, as much as the reflection on the language used to evoke that presence.

If we learn about the aid agencies, it is not their ubiquity that makes the impact, but the clothing of the description in these particular personalized reflections that makes the writer's agency visible:

> Now, my own rule of thumb is that any African country crawling under the weight of the white jeeps of postcolonial dependency is in trouble. It means that the modernity you see all around you is contrived, fragile, and artificially propped by ways and means that do not belong to you. It means that somebody somewhere is desperate for a narrative, for a showpiece, and is pouring resources and symbols into a particular space to prop it up as that showpiece and produce a desired narrative.

What marks these essays is not the features of a "counter-narrative," but rather a "pro-narrative" of delight, that leaves us in the embrace of Adesanmi's chuckles, his headshakes, and his own pleasure in giving us the glass case that matters, the one in which the exhibit is that of the marvelous speaker himself. He proclaims his own agency in speaking out. He claims an ownership over these words, and presents them, ultimately, as a challenge to his audience—in this case graduate students attending Michigan State University's Africanist Graduate Research Conference in 2014:

> What do these scenarios portend for you as graduate students and scholars of Africa? For starters, it means that the disciplinary space between elation and depression has not been fully probed in terms of our efforts to understand the dynamics of that continent. It means that we are yet to account for the elusiveness of agency and we do not even fully understand why it remains elusive and perpetually beyond grasp in Africa. If we do not understand why we lack agency, we will never find our way to it.

The challenge in each one of these essays returns to this point. I would not say it was so much to understand a lack, but to affirm that the locus of real agency is to be found within all those sources of elation he describes for us, really inviting us to answer the question posed by Jean-Pierre Bekolo in *Aristotle's Plot:* "what we don't got?" You want movie plots, we got. You want actors, words, dance, laughter, we got. And Adesanmi would add on, you want agency, you want stories? We got.

Most of all, Adesanmi defines himself as belonging to the generation for which it was not so much revolt, counter-narratives or counter-discourses, but an embrace, a mad embrace of its world—call that world "Nigeria"—echoed in the craziness of a lover's scream:

> Every generation had ways of imagining Nigerian newness, of imagining Nigeria newly. My generation screamed that Nigeria can be loved beyond reproach because we are bound to her by blood. But we also screamed that love for her must never imply limiting our creative energies and imagination to chronicling and narrativizing her. We found ways to extend her into the world in a postmodern actuation of the transnational imperative.

Like Uche Nduka, Adesanmi clearly places this reflection of himself and his generation in Uche's poetic achievement:

> After the chronicle of the life of my generation that he offered in the cinematic clip strategy of *Chiaroscuro* (1997), it is safe to say that Uche went on to embrace the world, fashioning a poetics unmoored in immediately localizable national anchors. The embrace of the world. The transnational imagination. The Afropolitan persona.

Here is where we finally come, in this collection: face-to-face with that persona of our times, he defines the next generation though its imaginary construction that reaches out to the personal and global:

> You encounter a new generation that must grapple with the identity politics of Afropolitanism and the attendant contradictions of trying to imagine a new Nigeria in an existential context which daily reminds them that the world is now their playground.

Although he stands aside, like an elder, from this new generation, it is in his characterization of its location that we can best describe his own exuberance: "the new generation [is] now animating and rocking the Nigerian literary scene."

His own ars poetica emerges in this beautiful declaration: "my generation had for raw material a Nigeria sapped beyond recognition by SAP and military rape and we tried out a poetics of love on her." Clearly, love is not so bad a means to situate oneself in the quest for an African agency.

Preface

Form as Resistance

The Story of This Book

In 2009, Penguin Books South Africa launched a new continental literary prize, the Penguin Prize for African Writing, "to highlight the diverse writing talent on the African continent and make new African fiction and nonfiction available to a wider readership." Penguin Books secured the imprimatur of Africa's foremost novelist, Chinua Achebe, who endorsed the prize. Two inaugural prizes would be awarded in fiction and nonfiction.

I was in Paris in the summer of that year, working on a manuscript, a collection of essays devolving from my thought and work as a peripatetic interpreter of the African imagination, and decided to enter the completed manuscript for the competition. In September 2010, I was awarded the inaugural Penguin Prize for African Writing in the nonfiction category at a grand ceremony in Johannesburg. The winning manuscript, *You're Not a Country, Africa,* was published a year later by Penguin Books. Zambian novelist, Ellen Banda Aaku, won in the fiction category with her novel, *Patchwork.*

Penguin Books South Africa was never able to sustain the project. The Penguin Prize for African Writing did not survive into a second edition. It became fixed in

Africa's literary history as a one-time continental prize won by a Nigerian and a Zambian. Nevertheless, for the two winning writers, the genie of fame had been let out of the bottle. Penguin Books organized a media blitz for us in South Africa. The media blitz spread to Europe and North America. Chinua Achebe's considerable influence helped. At every point during the award ceremony, Penguin Books let it be known that they had partnered with Achebe to inaugurate the prize. A statement authored by him was read at the event. Our published winning books, *You're Not a Country, Africa* and *Patchwork,* featured his signed statement as preface.

The prize had a dual consequence for me in terms of increased visibility in the public sphere and in the more restricted circuitries of African knowledge production in the academy. I was already a well-known syndicated columnist and public intellectual in Nigeria, and the prize increased my stock considerably in Africa's largest space of public intellection. In North American academe, I was an ascendant literary and cultural scholar with a very modest claim to name recognition in the circuits of African(ist) thought.

My only claim to disciplinary impact at the time was the fact that I had coauthored with the literary critic, Chris Dunton, a series of essays in the late 1990s–early 2000s in which we were signaling and theorizing the works of an emergent generation of Nigerian writers in a wave we labeled "third generation Nigerian writing." Nobody in North American academe was paying attention to little-known names like Chimamanda Ngozi Adichie, Helon Habila, Chris Abani, Teju Cole, Sefi Atta, Sarah Oladipo Manyika, Lola Shoneyin, and the generation of 1990s Nigerian poets whose poetic opus in Ibadan, Nsukka, and Lagos constitutes the background for the novelistic effervescence of the 2000s. Chris Dunton and I, lone voices in the wilderness, wrote and theorized this generation, editing special issues of *English in Africa* and *Research in African Literatures* along the way. When these writers exploded globally, our work became the foundational critique of a new generation of Nigerian writers.

The Penguin Prize for African Writing transformed me from a modest scholar and critic of third generation Nigerian writing to a more consequential figure in African thought. I returned to Canada from the award ceremony in Johannesburg to a plethora of keynote lecture invitations in Canadian, US, and European universities. Lecture invitations in Africa soon matched and outstripped a punitive schedule on the Canadian and US lecture trails. Suddenly, I was no longer attending academic conferences, workshops, and symposia as a self-sponsored panelist but as an invited keynote or featured speaker.

And the platforms were prestigious—Stanford, Vanderbilt, London School of Economics, etc. Invitations to address think tanks and policy outfits soon combined with strictly scholarly and academic lectures to produce quite an eclectic, trans-generic mosaic of thought and reflection on the African condition. In the first five years after the prize, I delivered more than forty keynote lectures in universities and other platforms in North America, Europe, and Africa.

I mention the trans-generic evolution of the body of work I was producing in my lectures because as a writer and scholar of literature and culture, I somehow also began to find myself in boardrooms and seminar rooms beyond the academy—the outcome of invitations to address Africa's three-piece suit–wearing, attaché briefcase–carrying hordes of policy wonks who preside over the fortunes of the continent by ferrying the latest data prepared in Western cathedrals of neoliberal, casino-capitalist thought—Brookings, McKinsey, Bretton Woods, and all that jazz. Whatever cookie cutter or ballpark version of Africa comes out of these places translates to the "indices," "growth," and "development indicators" stored in PowerPoint in the attaché briefcases of Africa's policy and political elite, ferried across the capital cities of the continent in meetings, seminars, workshops, and convenings, often featuring star appearances by Africa's partners from the Fund or the Bank.

In such gatherings where suited participants traffic in the hardware language of empirical data, GDP, growth, indicators, etc., I would be asked to bring in the software language of culture. My brief, usually, was to help the gathering think through the role and space of "African culture" (I usually would tell the audience that I prefer "the cultures of Africa") in the multiple agendas and visions that the continent's political and economic leaders were mapping for the twenty-first century. Often, I would feel like Chinua Achebe who was invited to address a meeting of the Organization for Economic Cooperation and Development (OECD) in Paris in 1989 and wrote famously about it in an essay, "Africa is People":

> I believe it was in the first weeks of 1989 that I received an invitation to an anniversary meeting—the twenty-fifth year, or something like that—of the Organization for Economic Cooperation and Development (OECD), in Paris. I accepted without quite figuring out what I could possibly contribute to such a meeting/celebration. My initial puzzlement continued right into the meeting itself. In fact, it grew as the proceedings got underway. Here was I, an African novelist among predominantly western bankers and economists; a guest, as it were, from the

world's poverty-stricken provinces to a gathering of the rich and powerful in the metropolis. (Achebe, 1999)

My foray into this world created a productive, auspicious tension in my writing. The language in which I had researched, written, and thought Africa in the seminar rooms of North America, first as a graduate student trafficking in postcolonial theory and postmodernism and, later, as faculty theorizing African and African Diasporic literatures and cultures on the pages of such eminent peer-reviewed journals as *Social Text, Comparative Literature, Modern Fiction Studies,* etc., had to find a meeting point between theoretical abstraction and empirical constriction in way that liberated my thought and work from both while benefiting from whatever I found useful and useable in the respective worlds.

By this time, I had also become a social media celebrity, followed on Facebook and Twitter by thousands across Nigeria and the rest of Africa. In a little over a decade, my Facebook Wall came to acquire the reputation of a public seminar room, attracting hundreds of African doctoral students, postdoctoral Fellows, and early-career faculty based in the continent, Europe, and North America. I was also writing prodigiously for that audience. Social media celebrity increased the pace of my public lectures in Nigeria, necessitating another mode of writing for a third category of audience.

Whether I was addressing the Stanford Forum for African Studies, Africa Talks at the London School of Economics, or doing keynotes at annual conferences of academic associations, the African Unity for Renaissance Conference of the Human Sciences Research Council of South Africa, or delivering public-oriented foundation addresses—Aga Khan Foundation, Awolowo Foundation—one thing was clear: while my subject matter was necessarily dictated by the theme of the event I was keynoting, I was always returning to the question of Africa's agency in the twenty-first century.

How may we conceptualize Africa in the driver's seat of her own destiny in the twenty-first century? How practically may her cultures become the foundation and driving force of her innovation, development, and growth in the age of the global knowledge economy? How may the Africanist disciplines in the humanities, the social sciences, and the natural sciences be revamped to rise up to these challenges through new imaginaries of intersectional reflection? As this theme—Africa's agency in the twenty-first century—evolved, albeit loosely and inchoately, in a decade of lectures delivered to academic and nonacademic audiences across three continents, other tensions arose for me.

Colleagues in the academic world were starting to notice the growing body of work contained in my lectures. The occasional encouragement to "put them together for publication" soon turned into sustained torrents of inquiries: have you revised and reworked them for publication? As the pressure to do a book mounted, I began to scrutinize and unpack the meaning of the constant advice I got to "revise and rework" the essays.

It soon became clear to me that virtually everyone who wanted to see the essays published had an understanding of "revise and rework" which boiled down to form and format. I would be advised to "tighten the essays" by cutting out "nonrelevant parts" to make them "more scholarly." As it were, the "nonrelevant parts" are areas where I deploy the full resources of African verbal artistry in the service of my message. In each lecture and for every audience, I had created a world in which form was completely indissociable from content.

The medium is the message, famously wrote Marshall McLuhan. His now cliché proposition comes close to theorizing what one obtains in African modes of discourse where epistemology and hermeneutics have meaning and validity only in the context of a performative interpellation of the collective body politic. No body of knowledge in *Things Fall Apart* or *Arrow of God* is dissociable from form: the verbal artistry of phatic communion and the performative architecture of discourse by Achebe's characters all combine to create a synergy of socialities and spiritualities in which knowledge inheres.

In this book, I have assembled lectures which reflect this indissociable union of form and content in my work. On the lecture podium, I have always sought to create an African world of signification in which verbal artistry interpellates performer and audience in a heuristic process of knowledge production. The African performative world that is pressed into service in these lectures is Yoruba. The narrative and delivery mode of the lectures, the antiphonal call and response, aspects of Yoruba oratory and verbal resources all combine with diction and borrowings from Nigerian popular culture to create a distinct African performative mode.

By keeping the exact mode and format in which each lecture was delivered, I not only invite the reader of this book into the full spectrum of the affective responses of the audience *in situ,* but I also hope that I am performing an act of resistance. In the last two years as I prepared this book and revised content as necessary, I came to resent the pressure to also revise form. There are certain disciplinary protocols of discourse and delivery—all Western—which confer the title of scholarship. In a book about Africa's agency, I was not going to revise and rework form to conform to Western ideals of the packaging, standardization, and delivery of knowledge. Form may very well be the next battle ground in Africa's long struggle for agency.

PART ONE

Crossfire

#WhoOwnsTheProblem?

Your Excellency President Thabo Mbeki, organizers, sponsors and cosponsors of this conference, esteemed colleagues, ladies and gentlemen, you must forgive me for the peculiar title of this lecture. It is true that the organizers of this timely conference gave me an unambiguous mandate about what they wanted me to do: share some reflections with you on the subject of finding African solutions for African problems. Specifically, they wanted me to engage the subject from the perspective of culture. Let me state from the onset that the singular, culture, is not my making. That is how it appears in my letter of invitation. Coming from a disciplinary background where the producer of knowledge must constantly watch out for traffic cops eager to hand out tickets for the offences of monolithization and essentialism, I probably wouldn't have dared to speak of an African culture in the singular purporting to solve African problems in the plural.

This keynote lecture was initially delivered as part of the opening plenary session addresses at the Fourth Annual African Renaissance for Unity Conference convened by the Africa Institute of South Africa and the Thabo Mbeki African Leadership Institute in Pretoria, South Africa, on May 22, 2014. A modified version of it was subsequently delivered as my valedictory lecture at the Institute of African Studies, University of Ghana, Legon, on May 29, 2014, in conclusion of my tenure as a Carnegie Diaspora Visiting Scholar.

However, not even the most audacious enforcers in all the humanistic and artistic disciplines with which we engage Africa would dare to hand out a traffic ticket to the scholar who drags the hashtag into the arena of serious scholarly reflection on the unending dilemmas of the African condition in the twenty-first century. These, indeed, are great times to be a hashtag. In my second life, I'd prefer to come back not as a bird or a flower as is the wont of nature lovers but as the world's most recognizable symbol, the hashtag, previously only known to Americans and the English as the pound key on their phones but catapulted to planetary celebrity status in a little under a decade by Twitter. The hashtag is the only subject that can legitimately claim to be more famous than Kimye—that conjugal combination of Kim Kardashian and Kanye West.

Indeed, it is not an exaggeration to describe the hashtag as the highest stage of globalization, what with its ability to go viral within seconds, crisscross geographical borders and ideological boundaries, connect cultures and peoples in defiance of difference, break down walls between causes and create a common village square for actors as far apart as gay rights activists of the Global North and anti-gay cultural fundamentalists of the Global South in Nigeria and Uganda, animal rights activists in Scandinavia and the whale and shark hunters of Japan, gender rights activists in the Global North and the bearded guys preventing women from driving in parts of the Arab world. Every time I reflect on this singular capacity of the hashtag to unite the world's largest community of strange bedfellows, I am almost always tempted to conclude that more than three decades of intense theorizing in the humanities and the social sciences have been reduced into a tiny symbol.

The intellection, which yielded world systems theory, globalization, and everything in between, and gave us illustrious cross-disciplinary thinkers of global flows, fluxes, and linkages such as Achille Mbembe, Mahmood Mamdani, Paul Tiyambe Zeleza, Adebayo Olukoshi, Thandika Mkandawire, Ato Quayson, Immanuel Wallerstein, Fredric Jameson, Edward Said, Arjun Appadurai, Gloria Anzaldúa, and so many usual suspects in the arena of contemporary global thought, now all boils down to the performative power of just one symbol: the hashtag. For the hashtag is world system, borderlessness, and globalization on steroids.

Some of you are already probably thinking that you know the reason why a Nigerian public intellectual would start an exercise such as this by singing the praise of the hashtag. Folks, don't blame me. My country, already a famous subject of all kinds of fair and unfair stereotyping here in Africa and the rest of the world, has seen her notoriety attain stratospheric heights courtesy of the hashtag. Doubtless some of you have already participated in what may now rightfully be termed a global hashtag movement. Perhaps some of you will take selfies in the course of this conference, brandishing a cardboard on which you would have inscribed the reigning marker of collective global activism: #BringBackOurGirls.

The phenomenal career of this particular hashtag—#BringBackOurGirls—has very obvious theoretical implications for those who have been thinking and theorizing the borderlessness of our postcolonial and postmodern world and the modes of Africa's insertion into it in the last three decades or so. But, more importantly, this conference will have to zoom in on the possessive adjective, "our," map its trajectory and modes of articulation, listen intently to its politics in order to determine who is speaking—or more appropriately, who has acquired the agency to speak—every time you encounter this celebrity hashtag.

In essence, this conference must ask the question: who is the "our" in #BringBackOurGirls? I don't know the answer but how you, esteemed colleagues, answer this thorny question will have very serious implications for the aims and goals of our gathering. For when I saw the theme of our conference, "African Solutions for African Problems," and the rider stating that more than a hundred scholars from Africa, Europe, and North America would gather here to find "African Solutions" to whatever we eventually agree—or agree to disagree—are "African Problems," my mind immediately went to #BringBackOurGirls (and even the Joseph Kony campaign before it), and I asked: Who owns the problem? Or, more appropriately, when was the last time Africa possessed the critical agency to own problems that are defined and narrativized as African? What are the possibilities of localizing the ownership of problems in the age of the hashtag? To make the inevitable allusion to Gayatri Spivak, can the subaltern own her problems?

Some of you may have noticed that no sooner had the #BringBackOurGirls handle gone viral than conflict over its origin and ownership arose, with CNN and the *Wall Street Journal* devoting time and space to clearing the air. And this war over ownership and narrative raged even as the girls were still in captivity. Who started it? Is it an offshoot of President Goodluck Jonathan's bring back the book campaign? Or is it more directly linked to Wole Soyinka's variation—with acknowledgment—on that presidential buzz with his own bring back the pupils retort? Or is it Oby Ezekwesili's making? Or is it the making of the American woman who immediately claimed ownership of it and rushed to edit her Wikipedia biography to include ownership of #BringBackOurGirls?

In the context of the politics—for there is always politics involved—of owning problems that are defined as African, it does seem to me that the advent of the hashtag and social media has introduced the dimension of separating the localized reality of problems from their modes of articulation, representation, and, I daresay, marketing. It seems to me that Africa is being told: you may own the scrawny children with countable ribs and mucus-soaked nostrils studying under baobab trees with chalkboards donated by UNICEF, we reserve the right to adopt those malnourished children with full media fanfare and scold you if you grumble—even if you are the president of a country like Malawi. You may own the lives and limbs being blown up in Kenya, in Congo, in Mali, and in the ungoverned Boko Haram territories of Nigeria; we own the glamor, glitz, and razzmatazz attendant upon the global dissemination and narrativization of those horrors.

This leads me to a second set of questions that must detain this conference. You may have noticed that I have been using the passive voice when talking about "African problems." In fact, I have avoided that particular phraseology employed by the conveners of the conference. Instead, I have been talking about "problems that are defined and narrativized as African." This mode of address is deliberate on my part. Apart from wondering whether Africa has the agency to own problems and their modes of articulation, the theme of this conference also made me wonder if we didn't need to problematize the problems before finding African solutions for them. Perhaps my unease is further heightened by the suspicion that a certain neoliberal sleight of the hand underwrites the expression, "African Problems." I believe the ability to smell neoliberal modes of framing, of naming, of engaging the actualities of Africa from a thousand miles come with the territory of what we do as the thinkers and writers of this continent. Hence, we must ask: What exactly are these African problems? How do problems acquire African citizenship? Who does the designation? When is it an African problem?

For anybody familiar with the usual laundry list, these questions may appear to be no-brainers. African problems? Oh, that's poverty, illiteracy, disease, hunger, comatose infrastructure, tribalism, bad governance, wobbly democracy and allied problems of leadership, crises and conflict, corruption, environmental degradation, the familiar tableau of human misery associated with the girl child, human trafficking and, above all, the failures of the postcolonial state—some would say her complete demission. This is by no means an exhaustive list of problems that have acquired African citizenship in global imaginaries of discourse. Each participant in this conference could draw up his or her own list, but I am sure we would have considerable overlaps. Consider, for instance, Professor Joseph Ki-Zerbo's list and see how close it is to mine:

> raging genocides, mass movements of refugees, tortures and mutilations, random destruction of the environment and bio-diversity, hostage-taking of the young generation as cannon fodder for warlords, the decimation of whole populations by pandemics, the stranglehold of the republican army, the giving away and eradication of age-old cultures and distinct knowledge.

Professor Ki-Zerbo's list of the pressing challenges of the continent obviously devolves from the register of wars, conflict, and crises. It is easy to run through the said list and think of Libya, Sudan, Somalia, Kenya, Nigeria, Mali, Congo, and all the ongoing hotspots in the continent—if one wasn't in the mood for immediate past specters of bloodletting in Rwanda, Liberia, and Sierra Leone. However, if you leave out any geographical referents, it is also quite possible for observers in other parts of the Global South to run through this generic list of problems that has acquired the tag, African, and assume that one was describing those places and spaces. What is there in my own list, for instance, that is not part of the politics of everyday life in significant parts of Southeast Asia, Latin America, and the Arab World?

Consider poverty. You'll be amazed by how comparable the indicators and the statistics are if you looked at, say, the situation in Peru, Honduras, Bangladesh, Ecuador, Papua New Guinea, Cambodia, the very black Deep South of the USA, the First Nations reservations of Canada, and Cameroon. Yet, only Africa becomes a synonym for these problems. The same applies to infrastructure. I've been reading that decrepit infrastructure is going to be one of the major headaches of the new Indian prime minister. The *New York Times* recently framed this problem, drawing on the capacity of Indians for self-deprecating humor. Indians, the newspaper claims, have a saying that while the English drive on the left of the road, Indians drive on what's left of the road. Booker Prize winner and activist, Arundhati Roy, also paints a grave picture of poverty and infrastructure in India in a post-election interview. Yet, that part of the register of underdevelopment that deals with dilapidated infrastructure is also almost always framed as an African problem.

These scenarios lead to some pressing questions. Do problems and human tragedies which also exist elsewhere become African because of perceived differences of spread and intensity? Do these problems become African because of imagined or real differences in the readiness of the institutions and opportunities of African modernity to rise up and solve them using critical human intelligence and innovation? Are these problems African because the websites of global actors in what I have previously theorized as the Mercy Industrial Complex (donor agencies, humanitarian organizations, aid and charity organizations, Bono, Jeffrey Sachs, career saviors of African children through adoption such as Madonna) almost always label them as African? More questions: do these problems become African because the continent is powerless against the modes of representation so powerfully captured by Binyavanga Wainaina in his classic piece, "How to Write about Africa"? There is even a latest variation of this problem of discursive and epistemological violence. I am told that there are particular ways to design the cover of the African novel, the African book, if you are a serious publisher looking for serious buyers of books about Africa in the Global North.

The acknowledgement by the organizers of this conference that culture has a role to play in finding African solutions for African problems is perhaps a conscious admission on their part that despite contemporary pressures to the contrary, history has a huge role to play in solving many of the said problems. To solve a problem is to understand it in all its manifestations and ramifications, and this includes its origins and modes of perpetuation. Yet, mentioning the colonial origin of many of the afflictions of the continent has become unfashionable in many of our disciplines. In my own discipline, it is taboo and could earn you a citation by the essentialism police.

As if Latin American thinkers like Aníbal Quijano and Walter Mignolo never theorized coloniality (the persistence in our present of the fault lines and effects of colonialism), you are told that the recourse to colonial paradigms to explain the benumbing dilemmas of the African present amounts to disciplinary laziness and an attempt to excuse, rationalize, or justify the self-imposed woes and tragedies of Africa. Yet, how could Mahmood Mamdani have explained Rwanda without going back to the colonial origins of the problem? How can I explain Boko Haram, how can I propose solutions to Boko Haram, without going back to 1914 in order to understand and map the errors of the rendering that have inevitably produced this gory Nigerian present? The search for more than two hundred school girls is only the latest stop in a journey programmed for tragedy and disaster by Lord Frederick Lugard in 1914. The Igbo genocide and the attendant civil war are also significant stops in that journey.

To recall Chinua Achebe, how do you begin the process of drying yourself when you are told that it is no longer fashionable to try and understand when, where, and why the rain began to beat you? How do you solve a problem when you are told that the ordained discursive procedure is to acknowledge and focus on your own contribution in making the rain that is beating you today and leave well enough alone with regard to yesterday's rain made by foreign rainmakers? Do these two epistemological propositions have to be mutually exclusive (Achebe, 1977)?

If history helps us to understand the origins and trajectory of many of the problems blighting the African present, culture is what explains why the problems became African or why outsiders of the neoliberal bent have been able to attach a fixed African identity to problems that are transcendentally human, even where we make allowances for differences of intensity. Culture is the location of the original injury of modernity. Culture was the first target of the discourses and the institutions of modernity at the moment of encounter. Many of the problems that Africa still has with the orders and institutions of modernity—democracy, governance, corruption, etc.—devolve from the unresolved contradictions of the original injury of modernity.

Let us not forget that modernity was imposed on the African largely through institutions of discipline and punishment, to borrow from Michel Foucault. The prison, the Christian mission, and the school did not stop at inflicting corporal punishment on the "African native" while scrupulously pursuing the civilizing mission; they equally all had very specific ideas about the cultures and worldviews of the African that we do not need to repeat here. If we need any reminder about this discipline-and-punish approach to the introduction of the structures of modernity in Africa, we need not look beyond the workings of the said institutions in Ferdinand Oyono's famous novel, *Houseboy.*

Thus, the African was culturally alienated from the institutions, protocols, and orders of modernity from the very start. This cultural alienation explains in large part the apathy to institutions, especially public institutions, in the continent. Institutions of modernity evolved as alienating structures of discipline and punishment under colonialism and have retained that identity in the postcolonial phase of African life. The postcolonial state has failed woefully in detaching itself and its institutions from the colonial socius of violence that birthed it.

Hence corruption! Hence the impunity with which the public till is plundered in so many African states, especially in my own Nigeria. As Kwame Gyekye (2013) reminds us in his book, *Philosophy, Culture, and Vision,* the cultural relationship of the African subject to his precolonial cultural and political community conduced to a collective ownership of institutions and modes of cultural citizenship which enhanced the notion of the common good. The communal stream, communal farmlands, communal institutions of governance and public order were not just in sync with the psychic world of the African subject; you took care of them because they commanded your loyalty and were not structures of violence and alienation.

Here then is the dilemma. Precolonial institutions, with all their warts and weaknesses, worked to a great extent and corruption was minimal—and punished adequately whenever it occurred—because those institutions acquired legitimacy and hegemony (as opposed to exercising only dominance and violence) through a historically developed sense of collective ownership. Postcolonial institutions have trouble working or functioning properly in Africa because they are orphans. Everybody steals from them; everybody leaves them to rot precisely because nobody owns them. The precolonial cultural attitudes of ownership of institutions and the collective good were never carried over because the new institutions destroyed or looked down upon the cultural values and worldviews that would have aided their insertion into the African space and psyche. These are contradictions that the modern African state has yet to resolve. She still hasn't been able to sell herself culturally to the African.

The story is told—and it is a true story—of the late Alhaji Bakin Zuwo, a governor of Kano State during the Second Republic in Nigeria, which lasted from 1979 to 1983. The task of making the daily trip to the public treasury to steal money became too cumbersome for this governor. To solve the problem, he introduced the practice of home delivery of stolen public funds into the lexicon of corruption in Nigeria. He simply had raw cash delivered to him in large quantities in his official residence which we call Government House in Nigeria. When the coup happened in 1983 and soldiers stormed Government House to arrest him, they were astounded by the quantity of raw cash they found in his bedroom. When queried, Bakin Zuwo famously quipped, "Government money in Government House, what is the problem?" This sums up the story of the African subject's conceptualization of the institutions of the postcolonial state. Would Alhaji Bakin Zuwo have had the same attitude to public office and to public property in the precolonial Emirate of Kano? Your guess, ladies and gentlemen, is as good as mine.

Like corruption and institutions, most of the problems and challenges that postcolonial Africa has encountered in the arena of democracy and governance can be explained on the ground of our radical departure from the economic and political cultures of precolonial Africa. All over the continent today, the state and her economy are hyper-centralized because they were carried over unmodified from the hyper-centralization of the political and economic structures of the colonial state. We are all familiar with the consequences of the hyper-centralization of political and economic power at the center all over the continent. It foreclosed the possibility of good governance and genuine democracy and facilitated the emergence of authoritarianism, supervised by the big man and his cronies.

Because the big man's cronies are almost always from his ethnic neck of the woods, tribalism enters the picture as the handmaiden of political and economic hyper-centralization. This has particularly been the case in much of Francophone Africa's postcolonial history, a period bloodied by the Father of the Nation and his single-party monolithism. This specter of hyper-centralized authoritarianism haunted the Francophone African novel of the 1970s and the 1980s, with novelists like Alioum Fantoure, Williams Sassine, Henri Lopes, Aminata Sow Fall, and Sony Labou Tansi leading the guard in the production of dictatorship novels. Wole Soyinka would respond in Anglophone Africa with *A Play of Giants.*

What sort of political and economic cultures did Africa evolve before the moment of colonial truncation? The case of the Igbo in eastern Nigeria is too well known to bear repeating here. Those of you who don't know Igbo republicanism in real life have encountered it in the political life of the six villages making up Umuaro in Chinua Achebe's (1964) *Arrow of God.* Gyekye (2013) has also explored what he describes as "consensual democracy" among the Ashanti and other ethnic groups in precolonial Ghana. I will therefore illustrate this part of my submissions with the precolonial political and economic cultures of my own people: the Okun people in the present Kogi state in Nigeria. Okun land is made up of a number of major towns around which gravitated hamlets and villages. Some of the major towns include Kabba, Mopa, Egbe, and my own Isanlu. Although the major traditional ruling stool was located in Isanlu, all the satellite villages and hamlets also had their own stools, which related in a traditional confederal fashion with the central stool in Isanlu.

Complementing this political confederacy was the fact that all the villages were economically autonomous and had their own independent markets and other economic structures. Colonialism destroyed this intricately decentralized political and economic culture and replaced it with the model with which we are all familiar. The postcolonial state completed the rout of Okun political and economic confederacy. Isanlu and all the adjoining villages and hamlets now had to start looking up to the local government, the state government, and the federal government in that order. I don't believe that we need to rehash the consequences of the collapse of the culture of confederacy and consensual democracy in Nigeria and elsewhere around the continent.

What needs to detain us here is the price that the continent continues to pay by stubbornly holding on to the machineries and institutions of political and economic centralization inherited from the colonial state instead of retracing her steps back to the precolonial cultural template in order to adapt, modify, and modernize it for contemporary usage. The first and perhaps most significant casualty of political and economic centralization is African innovation. The contest for resources at the center has stunted African innovation because we have evolved a culture in which an entire nation is fixated on just that one source of prebendal patronage. A rapacious political elite very often enlists the help of a confused intellectual class to think and theorize programs aimed at the consolidation of the current arrangement. For instance, Nigeria's erstwhile military dictator, General Ibrahim Babangida, was notorious for his generous use of professors to theorize and legitimize his policies.

Yet, recent developments in the continent point to the continued relevance of culture to any idea of renaissance and innovation. It is no longer a secret that Nigeria recently rebased her economy and announced her new status as Africa's largest economy, a distinction which promptly earned her the hosting rights for the recently concluded World Economic Forum Africa (WEFA). I am a man with an ear to the ground here in South Africa so I was made to understand that the news of being overtaken by Nigeria—with her premedieval infrastructure and epileptic power supply—was considered a huge joke in this country. I am told that you received that news like a rude slap in the face. You are not alone. Those of us who are consistent critics of the Nigerian establishment also took the same tack. However, reality is reality: Nigeria is Africa's largest economy, and culture played a significant role in the attainment of that feat. What went into Nigeria's rebased economy were the IT revolution and the cultural innovation represented by Nollywood and the Nigerian music industry. Just two decades ago, in the 1980s and 1990s, the party scene, the dance-floor scene, in this continent was dominated by American rap and R & B. On university campuses all over the continent, Michael Jackson, Janet Jackson, Mariah Carey, R Kelly, 112, Next, Changing Faces, Joe, and Boyz II Men reigned supreme. I particularly liked rocking in the nightclubs to the tune of 112's (1996) "Only You." Some of you may remember the lyrics. Do you? Why don't I give you the first line, and you sing along with me if you do: "Ohhhh I, need to know, where we stand . . ."

And how about this one, "End of the Road," from Boyz II Men in 1991. I am sure you still remember. Let me hear you: "Although we've come to the end of the road..."

Great! I have people with good R & B creds in this audience. These are great memories of the ancient times of the 1990s on the dance floors of Africa. Today, there has been a cultural revolution on dance floors and party halls across Africa. Whether you are in Belle Aroma nightclub where I unwind most weekends in Accra or you are checking out Lagos, Nairobi, Kampala, Monrovia, or Cotonou by night, the new cultural gospel is called azonto, skelewu, eminado, and dorobucci. Let me treat you to a YouTube clip of dorobucci so you can have a taste of what we are talking about. Ladies and gentlemen, these Anglophone African musical styles, along with Francophone African offerings such as "couper decaler," "mapouka," and "sagacite," have checkmated American musical imperialism on the African dance floor. And this cultural revolution has had such a seismic consequence in the arena of political economy that Nigeria quite almost literally danced her way to the top spot as Africa's largest economy. I guess you can tell from my familiarity with the latest grooves from the nightclubs of the capital cities of the continent that some of us are deconstructing and funkifying the image of the professor.

There are two lessons to be drawn from these scenarios. Culture is where Africa was written out of modernity; culture is where her development, genius, and innovative spirit were discounted. Culture is where her path to self-recovery is located. Cultural innovation is where Nigeria came into its own as Africa's largest economy and also joined Mexico, Indonesia, and Turkey in the MINT economies. Nigeria has no infrastructure fit for the nineteenth century; she can hardly generate a week's supply of electricity, and corruption is stratospheric. Yet, cultural innovation intervened and saved Nigeria's behind when it mattered most.

Secondly, you are nothing if you cannot even own and narrate your own problems. You are nothing if you are a fringe player in the global theater of naming and ascription. Those who name your problems for you will prescribe neoliberal solutions that fly in the face of your realities. As we have seen, the instruments for a global narrativizing of what constitutes African problems are cultural: social media—that is, Twitter, Facebook, Instagram, LinkedIn, MySpace, etc.—and, of course, print and broadcast media.

Problems are essentially African and not human problems because global culture names them so. It does not mean that Africa does not have and suffer disproportionally from the said problems. However, losing the means to own, narrativize, and engage your problems on your own terms is a double jeopardy. I am also not proposing Africa's isolation from the arena of bilateral and multilateral solutions to problems in this age of globalization and interdependence. Solutions would be skewed if problems are owned, narrativized, and skewed on your behalf. It is only through a conscious "rebasing" of culture, that is, a re-creation and owning of culture in the twenty-first century that Africa will be able to identify, name, and engage her own problems on her own terms.

Culture, Development, and Other Annoyances

Sawubona!

Doubtless, when this keynote lecture was advertised and you saw the last keyword, "annoyances," in the title, some of you wondered why the conveners of this prestigious lecture series decided to settle for an angry Nigerian public intellectual based temporarily in Ghana. Some of you may have wondered still: What's biting the Nigerian professor? Why is he annoyed? We, South Africans, ought to be the ones screaming out our annoyance, having only been recently eliminated from the early stages of the African Nations Championship by his country—and on our own turf to boot! Fortunately, as I am not used to gloating about Nigeria's continental football superiority, especially in the presence of our football younger brothers such as Ghanaians, Cameroonians, Egyptians, and South

---

This keynote lecture was delivered in Johannesburg at the International Leadership Platform Conference convened jointly by the University of Johannesburg and the Africa Institute of South Africa (AISA) on February 19, 2014. On February 20, 2014, it was presented as a cultural diplomacy seminar at the Diplomatic Academy of South Africa's Department of International Relations and Cooperation in Pretoria, at the instance of Anesh Maistry, deputy director, Foreign Service. On February 28, 2014, a version of it was delivered as a public lecture convened by the Department of English, University of Ghana, Legon.

Africans, let me quickly assure you all that I may be annoyed alright, but it's got absolutely nothing to do with continental rivalries in football.

My annoyance—or annoyances, pardon the untidy plural—has also got nothing to do with the fact that I had less than two weeks to prepare and write this lecture, tucking it into the grind of other forthcoming keynote lectures in Nigeria and Canada next week. On the contrary, let me reassure the masquerade behind that punitively short-notice invitation, Dr. Pinkie Mekgwe, executive director of internationalization, University of Johannesburg, that she taught me a valuable lesson when she sent that invitation in a tone that made it clear to me that she was not going to take no for an answer.

"You must come," Pinkie had written before describing how prestigious this particular lecture platform is! It then dawned on me that if I was being asked to literally hop on the next flight and come down here to Johannesburg for this lecture, Pinkie was intimating me with the fierce urgency of the business of Africa. She was telling me that there can be no such thing as a short notice in our collective duty as writers, scholars, and intellectuals to write, think, and envision a future for this continent NOW! She was telling me that only the permanently ready thinker is worthy of the privilege of getting his or her hands dirty in the vineyards of Africanist knowledge production. Thanks to Dr. Mekgwe and how she ambushed me for this lecture, I now know that the famous motto, "Be Prepared," belongs more to those who are called upon to think and write Africa than it belongs to Baden Powell and his Boy Scouts movement.

I am therefore immensely grateful to Dr. Mekgwe for the invitation and the epistemological teachable moment that came along with it. I am grateful to the University of Johannesburg's International Leadership Platform, and cohosts, the Africa Institute of South Africa (AISA) for the honor and privilege of being asked to come and share my reflections with you—and, alas, my annoyances! Thanks are due to the respondent, Professor Peter Vale, for agreeing to this task even at the risk of not receiving the lecture until a few hours to delivery! Finally, I want to thank you all, distinguished members of the audience, for "taking time out of no time" (as we say in Nigerian English) to attend this lecture. Seeing you all here reminds me of the ties that bind, of why I love visiting your beautiful country for I've been here for one and the repeated time since the 1990s.

This great country of yours is the site of the last great African anger and annoyance provoked by the fundamental unjustness of man to man (apologies to Bob Marley). You, South Africans, led your country, Africa, and the global community of conscience against this historical unjustness by articulating a struggle powered not just by the bombs of "Umkhonto we Sizwe"; the global resonance of your uprisings and wars against the apartheid machine (Sharpeville); the spectacular trajectories of your great anti-apartheid heroes and sheroes (Steve Biko, Nelson Mandela, Albert Luthuli, Robert Sobukwe, M. D. Naidoo, Desmond Tutu, Michael Hermal, Winnie Mandela, Ruth First, and countless others); but also, and more importantly, a struggle rooted in and nourished by a deontology of culture.

In essence, your worldview, your way of life, your stories, your memory, what you thought of beauty and ugliness and how you expressed those aesthetic sentiments, how you laughed, how you loved, how and what you ate, how and what you sang, and how you danced all came together to constitute the soul of your struggle. If there is anything to be learned from the documentary movie *Amandla* (2002), it is that you did not just fight apartheid to a standstill; you danced and sang that tragedy to its ignominious end, and, in doing so, you taught the rest of us, your admirers around the world, that the unfathomable zone of potential and becoming we commonly refer to as a people's future cannot be envisaged or envisioned outside of their culture, understood in the broadest, evolving, and most dynamic sense possible.

Precisely because your future as the Rainbow Nation was secured at the price of a long-drawn struggle nurtured by your culture, by who you are; precisely because yours was the last great continental affirmation of the significance of culture—among other things—to the emergence of statehood from colonial debris, you are auspiciously positioned to understand the dilemmas and the discontents framing current discussions of the role of culture in shaping the future of a continent whose friends and enemies agree is on the cusp of yet another historical moment. Having now shaken off the last yoke of colonial domination in 1994, the argument goes roughly, Africa must quit the path of blaming outsiders for her numerous challenges and begin to start being responsible for her present and future.

The morphology of this future and what exactly it would take to get us there is where the tough cut lies. Often, we get mixed signals from friends and foes alike. After 1994 and at the beginning of the new millennium in 2000, *The Economist,* for instance, ushered Africa into the twenty-first century with the now infamous cover title, "Africa: The Hopeless Continent." A little over a decade later, this mouthpiece of Western capitalist paternalism changed its tune and declared Africa a hopeful continent. This proclamation came in the context of a world suddenly gone gaga about the prospects of the African continent. The international capital and finance community, the development community, the global NGO and activist community, and world governance bodies and their continental appendages in Africa, as well as the institutional and disciplinary world of the social sciences, began to crowd the global space of discourse with dizzying statistics and data bearing narratives of growth and sustainable development; of GDP and capital flow; of governance and democracy. Ghana and Botswana were placed in showrooms as examples of Africa rising.

I spoke earlier of mixed signals. Let us not forget that despite this shift from Afro-pessimism to Afro-optimism by the global determiners of growth and progress, when it came to the acronyms they invented to describe who was rising, growing, or emerging in the Global South, Africa was accorded little or no space. Thus, we got the BRIC countries into which South Africa was admitted as an afterthought, a tagalong, to give us BRICS. And now I hear that we have the MINT countries. My own Nigeria thankfully made the cut this time. I think there has been a deliberate attempt here to put South Africa in BRICS and Nigeria in MINT. Put them in the same room and their rivalry will bring down the roof! There are also the famous Next-11 countries. Here, Egypt makes the cut. In essence, the gale of post–new millennium Afro-optimism from the North will only allow three of fifty-four countries into its nirvana of acronyms.

Whatever the signals, clear or mixed, one thing informed these projections into Africa's future. Whether those making such robust projections loudly are latter-day converts to Afro-optimism of *The Economist* or neo–Bretton Woods variety or technocrats and development experts speaking in those familiar growth, democracy, and good governance talkshops from Davos to Addis Ababa; from the boardrooms of corporate Africa to the seminar rooms of the continent's universities, we are told that Africa's future is bright because of the boundless energy, genius, and creativity of her youth demographic.

The oldest continent, we are told, presents the ironic scenario of having the greatest number of young people on earth. This youth demographic is said to be opportunity. All that needs to be done now is for the African state to place the millennium development goals within the reach of this vast youth demographic, pursue infrastructural renewal and economic growth and expansion, eradicate the unholy trinity of poverty, ignorance, and disease, deepen democracy and good governance, and all other things shall be added.

Going by the tenor and body language of the African Union, that body certainly believes that the path to Africa's future lies somewhere in the philosophy of the development community as I have sketched it out above. I should know. The African

Union has been working on a vision roadmap for the continent as some of you here probably know. The fiftieth anniversary of the OAU in 2013 inspired the African Union to try to project into the next fifty years and determine what the continent would look like. The AU spent much of 2013 organizing talkshops all over the world. From academia to the corporate world, stakeholders in the future of the continent were asked to reflect on Africa in the next fifty years. The idea was to eventually produce some kind of Africa 2063 document—a roadmap for the continent in the next fifty years. I was privileged to be part of that process, alas, the culmination but not the origin of my annoyances in this onerous business of thinking Africa.

To draft a 2063 agenda for the entire continent, the AU needed to consult very widely. Inevitably, these consultations involved Africans of the old and the new Diaspora. The AU wanted both categories of Diaspora Africans to contribute to drafting this all-important document that would have been produced by Africans at home and abroad about the future of our beloved continent. Thus it was that in October 2013, I had the extraordinary privilege of being invited to New York by the African Union to be part of the Diaspora Consultations meeting on the Africa 2063 agenda. Our brief during the said meeting in New York was unambiguous: we were asked to project into the future, as far ahead as 2063, to encounter the Africa of our dreams. We were asked to engage the question: what Africa would you love to see in 2063?

As I contemplated the theme of that meeting in my apartment in Accra, prior to departure for New York, I thought it was dangerous business to gather academics, technocrats, and bureaucrats in New York and ask them to envision Africa fifty years down the road. I thought that the AU was in a way asking us to encroach on the coveted territory of prosperity Pentecostal pastors who have taken over the entire continent and are assuring Africa's one billion people that next year, and the year after the next, until we get to 2063, shall be the year of their miracle and abundance. My apprehension was further deepened by certain developments. After being told that I would be addressing a plenary session of the New York meeting from the perspectives of culture and identity, I sat on the patio of my residence on the campus of the University of Ghana, a cup of coffee in hand, and tried to start reflecting on the subject that was taking me to New York.

However, I had difficulty concentrating on that task because just across the road from me, an open-air campus-for-Jesus prosperity Pentecostal crusade was rounding up a week of intense miracles and testimonies and the participants in that spiritual revelry were determined that the huge loudspeakers they had deployed for the occasion would cause an earthquake on campus and around Accra, so loud was the noise of the singing, the ministration, and the anointing. As I was blogging about the event on my Facebook Wall, the officiating pastor said something I'm sure all of you in this room have heard before.

It is something I have encountered in country after country as I have crisscrossed the African continent in the last two decades as a writer and a student of the evolving cultures and identities of the youth of Africa. It is something that has made me arrive at the conclusion that prosperity Pentecostalism, along with its cultures, styles, and modes of social inflection, is now the most significant cultural wind blowing across the continent, rivalled perhaps only by the social media revolution. The pastor in Accra asked his audience to close their eyes. Then he thundered: "next year, *Forbes* magazine will release another list of the wealthiest Africans. If you can see yourself in that list, please stand up and scream for Jesus." The resultant decibel level from his audience shocked and awed me. I assure you, you can't make these things up.

We were in October 2013. The image of nearly one thousand undergraduates of the University of Ghana screaming in Pentecostal jouissance, assured that they would appear in the January 2014 edition of *Forbes* magazine as Africa's newest billionaires, is what I took with me the following day to board the Delta Airways flight which took me to the African Diaspora consultation meeting on the Africa 2063 Agenda of the AU in New York. On board, I thought about it all. All we need do to have an idea of Africa in 2063 is listen to the continent's prosperity Pentecostal pastors as they enrapture hundreds of millions of our citizens from Kenya to Zimbabwe, Nigeria to Tanzania, Ghana to Namibia, Congo to Cameroon, Uganda to South Africa, and our job would be largely done. Africa in 2063 would be littered with *Forbes*-rated billionaires flying private jets.

Although I would very much have loved to claim all the promises and miracles of prosperity Pentecostalism for Africa and Africans by the year 2063, I had other agendas in mind as I boarded the plane for New York. I was going to do a plenary on what role culture might play in Africa's march to 2063. I thought that what I witnessed in Accra would be a good entry point for an auspicious discussion of the power, appeal, and relevance of culture to any discussion of Africa's future.

Beyond faith, Pentecostalism has morphed into a powerful subculture across the continent, affecting every aspect of life, from governance and democracy, to the diction and worldview of a significant proportion of the continent's youth. The language of development and post-development, with its long list of sustainable this and that, industry, technology, innovation, economic expansion, science, technology, and all the usual suspects presupposes a citizenry ready to travel along those paths under the guidance of a visionary leadership. What happens when a significant proportion of this citizenry evolves in a mainstreamed subculture of immediate miracles? Can Africa's planners and policy makers afford to ignore this and allied cultural forces now shaping African identities as they project into the future?

I did not get the chance to make these submissions in New York. Indeed, I had very little time to situate culture as a key plank in the envisioning process being undertaken for the continent. Unlike all the other plenary presenters who were allotted fifteen-minutes individually for their presentations, I discovered at the venue of the event that two of us had been lined up for the segment on reflections on culture. Worse, we had to cram our respective presentations into a fifteen-minute slot, a fact we both found out only at the very moment of presentation. Evidently, the African Union, like the continent's technocrats, bureaucrats, planners, policy makers, and political leaders, is persuaded by the thinking that the hardware language of growth and development, of macro and microeconomics, of cutting-edge technology and industry, of GDP and other dizzying data from the IMF, the World Bank, the African Development Bank, and relevant agencies of the UN, is more germane to the continent's advancement than the software language of culture.

It dawned on me painfully in New York that whenever two or three development experts are gathered in the name of Africa's future, culture is always invited as a sideshow, as entertainment. The development experts and data wielders in New York would have been content if I had made a presentation on Nollywood as momentary diversion from their very serious business of thinking Africa and her future as statistical numbers to be crunched. For them, GDP, growth data, and development statistics were the path to that future. No need to understand the cultures, subcultures, and countercultures informing the imaginaries and identities of that much-touted youth demographic and how such cultures might shape destination 2063.

If I was annoyed by the peripheral space allotted to the possible role of culture in Africa's future and development during the New York plenary sessions, more annoyance(s) awaited me on my return to Accra. This time the event was a book launch attended by the usual suspects: diplomats, technocrats, bureaucrats, academics, and the like. As it happens, discussions were lively and engaged. Then I asked a question about history and culture. A diplomat responded that we've had enough of "this history and culture stuff" and what we need now are science, technology, and accelerated development. We were in the Institute of African Studies where that response ought to have struck everyone as odd. As no one flagged it, I did not want to be forward, being a visitor. I let it pass but filed it in my memory as one of those instances where culture is seen as an obstacle to development. My ilk and I often feel a sense of alienation in such development gatherings.

My ilk? I am talking about those of us working as writers, scholars, and activists in the continent's arts and culture establishment, lone voices screaming in the wilderness, struggling to persuade Africa's bureaucrats, technocrats, planners, state officials, and policy makers that they labor in vain if they continue to give a short shrift to culture as they map Africa's path to her future and destiny. I am sure you understand that there were other annoyances before my own recent histories of annoyance at being constantly invited to meetings and development talkshops in Africa and outside of the continent where culture is meant to entertain neoliberal think tank types trafficking all day long in GDP data and statistics funded largely by our friends in Bretton Woods. I am sure you all remember Ngugi wa Thiong'o and his lifelong frustration and annoyance over the language question in Africa. Ngugi's case is too familiar to bear repeating here.

But we must mention the less familiar case of Chinua Achebe. He too was down that road in the 1980s, and he reminds us in the essay, "Africa Is People." Like my humble self in New York, Chinua Achebe had the misfortune of being among development experts in one of those meetings where Africa is somehow expected to develop outside of her cultures. Says Achebe (1999):

> I believe it was in the first weeks of 1989 that I received an invitation to an anniversary meeting—the twenty-fifth year, or something like that—of the Organization for Economic Cooperation and Development (OECD), in Paris. I accepted without quite figuring out what I could possibly contribute to such a meeting/celebration. My initial puzzlement continued right into the meeting itself. In fact it grew as the proceedings got underway. Here was I, an African novelist among predominantly western bankers and economists; a guest, as it were, from the world's poverty-stricken provinces to a gathering of the rich and powerful in the metropolis. As I listened to them—Europeans, Americans, Canadians, Australians—I was left in no doubt, by the assurance they displayed, that these were the masters of our world, savouring the benefits of their success. They read and discussed papers on economic and development matters in different regions of the world. They talked in particular

about the magic bullet of the 1980s, structural adjustment, specially designed for those parts of the world where economies had gone completely haywire.

Eventually, Chinua Achebe did have his eureka moment:

> Suddenly I received something like a stab of insight and it became clear to me why I had been invited, what I was doing there in that strange assembly. I signalled my desire to speak and was given the floor. I told them what I had just recognized. I said that what was going on before me was a fiction workshop, no more and no less! Here you are, spinning your fine theories, to be tried out in your imaginary laboratories. You are developing new drugs and feeding them to a bunch of laboratory guinea pigs and hoping for the best. I have news for you. Africa is not fiction. Africa is people, real people. Have you thought of that? You are brilliant people, world experts. You may even have the very best intentions. But have you thought, really thought, of Africa as people?

Out of annoyance, Ngugi wa Thiong'o screams that Africa is language. Out of annoyance, Chinua Achebe screams that Africa is people. Language. People. Culture. You begin to wonder why those experts and technocrats who insist that Africa's youth bulge is an opportunity also insist on not seeing the nexus between youth cultures and the future of the continent. You wonder why political leaders across the continent insist on the false dichotomy between science and technology on the one hand and culture on the other hand. In my own country, Nigeria, for instance, the scramble for science and technology (alias accelerated development) attained such a maddening frenzy that policies were put in place to discourage arts subjects, which came to be seen as obstacles to development. Politicians began to openly denigrate the teaching of African history, cultures, and languages in our schools.

This is what renowned Nigerian historian, Professor Toyin Falola, refers to as "the persecution of the arts and humanities" in African educational systems by bureaucrats and officials of state keen on the teaching of science and technology and development-oriented subjects. By doing this, the state creates a dichotomy and a false hierarchy between science and technology on the one hand and arts and culture on the other hand. Says Falola (2012):

> Here comes the bad news for the persecutors. Creating, managing, and solving underdevelopment is a human cultural concern. And this is where the humanities

come to the fore as they generate greater imagination, thereby creating more intellectual creativity, encouraging broader reflection on the future of society.

The university in my own part of Africa is of course not left out of this persecution business. If you look at recent vision documents by some leading universities on the continent, you will detect the underhand privileging of certain disciplines in response to the funding priorities of the World Bank. I believe I don't need to tell you which disciplines are being de-emphasized and which ones are being privileged and narrativized as being more germane to Africa's growth and development by the concerned universities.

The complicity of the African university with this scenario is one frustrating source of annoyance, for this is the site where the critical connections between culture, science, and technology ought to be made. The gown ought to make these connections and persuade the town to see them. I don't know how much of Kwame Nkrumah's (1964) great essay, "The African Genius," you all remember. That essay was the keynote address he delivered at the founding of the Institute of African Studies, University of Ghana, on October 25, 1963. While giving the new institute a mandate to tie culture to development (and not separate them as is annoyingly done today), Nkrumah indicates that the premium that he and his generation of African leaders placed on culture stems from their understanding of the fact that growth, development, science, and technology all depend on a people's creative genius, which, in turn, depends on taste.

Taste is a function of culture. Taste is a matter of aesthetics. What a people consume and how they consume it depend entirely on their cultural lifeworld. Innovation, science, and technology respond to taste as shaped by culture. Twitter was invented because somebody somewhere understood America's cultural obsession with information that could be packaged and consumed quickly like fast food. Innovations in the automobile industry are entirely driven by years of field surveys into taste as driven by culture. This is the meeting point of technology, development, and culture. Africa's science and technology in the future will be driven by the cultural tastes and predilections of the peoples of Africa.

If Nkrumah could see these connections in 1963, why have things become so hazy in 2014? If these connections are not being made today by the African University, if certain disciplines and fields are being privileged while others are "persecuted" in response to the funding stimulus of the World Bank and such other bodies and agencies in the Global North, is there any wiggle room for strategic critique and remedial actions? Is there any agential location from which one could resist the ideological preferments of those who pour millions into the preservation of the cultures, tastes, and ways of life of the Global North, preserving culture and the arts, funding museums and other locations of culture and memory, only to turn around and tell you that your own culture is antithetical to science, technology, and development? As our friend, Binyavanga Wainaina, recently puts it, how does one imagine "the new" or "newness" in Africa when the very paradigms of imagining are defunded, discouraged, and stigmatized as inimical to progress, growth, and development?

The problematic of newness, of imagining the new in Africa, brings us back to the question of the youth bulge and what that demographic phenomenon portends for the future of the continent. As I stated earlier, policy makers, bureaucrats, and experts in the development community bandy data and statistical figures ranging from 60 percent to 70 percent youth demographic for many African countries, with youth sometimes defined as persons thirty years old and below. Whichever way one looks at it, the majority of Africa's one billion people fall within the youth demographic. Using conventional language and its assorted registers—GDP, growth, development agendas, plans, etc.—Africa's bureaucrats and development experts pay attention to everything about this particular demographic except for their cultural predilections and predicament.

Yet we forget that their peers in America have invented Facebook, Twitter, Instagram, and Pinterest in response to specific cultural imperatives and stimuli; we forget that their peers in China, Japan, South Korea, and other parts of Asia are in a daily competition to invent apps informed by the cultural circumstances of those places. In essence, the youth of other continents are meeting the world, unleashing their genius and creativity on the rest of the world from the platform of their respective cultures. On what cultural platform are the youth of Africa expected to meet the world and compete with their peers when, as stated earlier, the teaching of African history, cultures, and languages is treated largely as an impediment to science and technology disciplines in many African school systems? Lack of sufficient attention to the power of culture can sometimes mean the difference between being the next Mark Zuckerberg or just another burden on Africa, eating grass in sheepish obedience to the instruction of your pastor while awaiting the immediate miracle of your millions tomorrow. I'm sure you all know a thing or two about this grass-eating business here in South Africa.

Something is awfully funny and I dare not conclude this lecture without mentioning it. Whether we are dealing with the politicians, technocrats, or bureaucrats in Africa, those who are loudest in disavowing the organic linkages between culture and science and technology; those who file criminal charges against culture, accusing her of being an enemy of progress and an obstacle to sustainable development, are the first to run for cover under the umbrella of culture the moment their comfortable prejudices are threatened. Think of the anti-gay legislations in Nigeria and Uganda and how the politics of it all has played out as a culture war between Africa and the West. All of a sudden, those who would have Africa shake off the shackles of culture and backwardness in order to embrace progress, science, and technology became custodians of "our culture." They spoke authoritatively in the name of culture, defined it, protected it, determined what it must include and exclude, and framed Africa as a puritanical cultural entity in opposition to the corroding influences of the West.

Culture was suddenly back in business! Beyond prejudice, beyond the tragedy of the politics of exclusion on account of a person's sexual orientation, there is a crucial point that has been overlooked in the back and forth between the protagonists and the antagonists of the gay laws in Nigeria and Uganda. Through slavery, through colonialism, through every manner of historical tragedy, the humanity of the African was questioned on the basis of his culture. The responses to these historical tragedies—Négritude, cultural nationalism, etc.—were mostly gestures of cultural affirmation. Today, the gay controversy reminds us that culture is still the site where Africa is being asked to provide evidence of her membership of the human family. Culture is also the site where Africa is pushing back, claiming rightly or wrongly to be resisting foreign imposition.

As 2014 came upon us, many technocrats and development experts across Africa momentarily dropped their GDPs, their data, their statistics, their micro and macroeconomic indicators, hoisted culture on their heads and went to war against the West in the name of culture! Now, ain't it amazing, as my favorite country music crooner, Don Williams, would put it?

For Whom Is Africa Rising?

(We just lost Professor Ali Mazrui. May we please
observe a minute's silence in his honor?)

The best of times and the worst of times. No, I have not come to Michigan
State University to conduct an excursion into quotable quotes from Charles
Dickens. I am just taking the liberty—presumptuously, some of you might
say—to put into words what it must feel like to wear that enigmatic title,
"Africanist scholar," in these most paradoxical of times for and on the continent.
One would ordinarily have assumed that being privileged to be called a producer
of knowledge about a part of the world which is said to possess the distinction of
being at once the cradle and future of humanity would come with the fringe benefit
of permanent elation.

There is one additional reason why permanent elation ought to be the defining
essence of my own interpellation as a producer of Africanist knowledge. In the
complicated business of nationalism and national identities in Africa, we learned a
few years ago—from one of those studies frequently purporting to have discovered
new truths about the African condition—that my own corner of the continent,
Nigeria, is home to the happiest people on earth. All one hundred and seventy

Keynote lecture delivered at the Eighth MSU Africanist Graduate Research Conference, East Lansing,
Michigan, October 17, 2014

million of us provide one jolly canvas of carnival, revelry, and jouissance. Now, we are talking about the largest group of Africans in one national place—indeed, the world's largest assembly of black people in a single nation-space—being uniformly happy in this trickle-down neoliberal world of ours. If Nigeria's happiness trickles down, chances are the remaining 1.1 billion less fortunate Africans will at least get reasonable drops of the happiness tonic.

A little over a billion happy Africans should be good enough reason for the intellectual, whose job it is to make disciplinary meaning of their ways and their world, to be permanently elated. The way I see it, happy subjects make happy scholarship, and happy scholarship makes the world go round! Wishes, sadly, are not horses. So we know that elation of a permanent kind is a risky proposition in the business of engaging Africa, especially in terms of her checkered trajectory in the struggle for agency. Permanent tornness between the diametrically opposed sentiments of elation and depression, as evoked in the Dickensian conundrum, is a safer emotional and psychological refuge for the student of Africa.

Okay, let's get depressed before we get elated! As you already know, our renowned Professor Ngugi wa Thiong'o did not win the 2014 Nobel Prize for Literature after yet another nomination round. Beyond the intellectual terrain, indeed, 2014 has been a very bad year for African sports. Virtually all our teams performed woefully in Brazil, producing a cavalcade of images leading dangerously back to the familiar routes of African stereotyping. Benoit Assou-Ekotto's head-butting of teammate Benjamin Moukandjo; the emergency plane load of dollars from the troubled economy of Ghana to placate players in full rebellion in Brazil; the repeated hints of threat and rebellion in the Nigerian camp are all texts underwritten by some unsayable ur-texts, constantly hinted at or whispered on social or traditional media: Africa's corruption and institutional demission. Note that the misbehavior of Luis Suárez remained the misbehavior of bad boy Luis Suárez and did not have transcendental or generic identity consequences for the American continent.

Let's have some more depression. As I prepared to board the plane in Ottawa, I received an email from notable African scholar Professor Paul Tiyambe Zeleza, vice president for academic affairs at Quinnipiac University. The crossover to administration was never going to slow down the constant flow of books and essays from Professor Zeleza's goatskin bag of wisdom. As it happens, some of us in his inner circle of friends do receive personal new essay alerts from him. The essay I received alerted Professor Zeleza's "Dear Friends" to the publication in Aficasacountry.com of his latest essay, entitled "Why I am Afraid of the African Disease of Ebola" (2014).

It is true that the continent moved from the great depression of Brazil in July to the deadly depression of Ebola in August. But I am sure that you can already take a stab at the drift of Zeleza's essay from the title. It's a satirical tour de force on the politics of yet another gigantic "single story" (apologies to Adichie) about Africa. Of course I have been preoccupied with the emotional roller coaster that is Ebola. After all, the outbreak in Guinea and Liberia occurred just as I prepared to leave Accra after a one-year stint as a Carnegie Diaspora Visiting Professor of African Studies at the University of Ghana, Legon. I've been part of a Nigerian social media community of mourning as precious lives were lost to Ebola. Beyond loss and trauma, Ebola is creating new economies of meaning, of contact, of cross-border figurations on the continent and of transnational calibrations of African identities across the Atlantic. I have been part of it all like everybody else.

What caught my attention in Zeleza's essay, therefore, is that after almost four decades of "writing back" through such milestones as Chinua Achebe's (1977) "An Image of Africa," Chinweizu's (1975) *The West and the Rest of Us,* Ngugi wa Thiong'o's (1986) *Decolonising the Mind,* Claude Ake's (1982) *Social Science as Imperialism,* V. Y. Mudimbe's (1988) *The Invention of Africa;* after Fanon, after Cabral, after Rodney, the usual prosecution witnesses have dragged yet another icon of African studies to the intellectual court to play the part of a defense lawyer and argue our case: that Africa is not Ebola and Ebola is not Africa. For I must say it unequivocally that Paul Tiyambe Zeleza speaks for me in that essay.

After every routine needless killing of a black male teenager by police in this country, I am sure you are familiar with the spectacle on cable television of black mothers lamenting the ritual of having to have "that talk" all over again with their black teenage sons over dinner: how to appear nonthreatening when pulled over by cops. Not again, such mothers gasp in exasperation. And you notice the weariness of the soul seared into those voices. A hint of that sentiment creeps in on me whenever circumstances force any of us to pick up his keyboard and reaffirm what Africa is not. Africa is not Ebola, Zeleza laments. And I experience a weariness of the soul that the ritual of enunciative disavowal of stereotype is once again foisted on us. That talk that we are not Ebola; that talk that we are not HIV/AIDS; that talk that we are not famine, hunger, war, and want. Over and over we must do it again and again. Sisyphus and his boulder have far better luck than Africa and the knowledges we generate to engage her in the theater of representation.

Still on depression, the 2014 Ibrahim Index of African Governance has been published as you all probably already know. The continent's performance is assessed under such rubrics as safety and rule of law, participation and human rights, sustainable economic opportunity, and human development. Whatever noticeable gains there are in the individual fortunes of particular countries are immediately dampened by the overall average result for the entire continent: 51.5 percent. That's a "D–" in the North American grading system, one rung of the ladder above an outright F: how else can one express the uninspiring performance!

I am sure you will all agree with me that no portrait of depressing points about Africa would be valid in which our friends in Bretton Woods didn't make an appearance. The last newsflash I read before I boarded the plane for the trip here announced that Ghana had started the final round of talks with the IMF on a bailout loan. The news came packaged in registers and diction which evoked the trauma of the 1980s when SAPs, conditionalities, market forces, market-driven shocks, economic downturn, devaluation, inflation, and austerity measures emptied the present of my generation across Africa and mortgaged our future. Three decades after the IMF laid the foundation of the realities which made our bosom friends in *The Economist* (2000) declare Africa a hopeless continent, Ghana, one of the few countries so often placed in a glass display case as continental success stories, is back at Bretton Woods, beaten, battered, and broke.

My generation came of age in the 1980s, writing tests and exams on foolscap sheets. Jacques de Larosiere and his successor at the IMF, Michel Camdessus, sealed our fate with policies rammed down the throat of one military dictator after another across the continent. Today, the youth who make Africa tick are on Facebook and Twitter grumbling about the size of the iPhone 6 even as Christine Lagarde declares enthusiastically that an appropriate "policy mix" will be worked out to ensure a "good bailout" for Ghana. I am of the '70s/'80s. A generation came of age in the '90s. Another came of age in the 2000s. Three generations of Africans, only one uniting factor: Bretton Woods's policy "mixes." With Christine Lagarde talking about Ghana in 2014 like Getafix the Druid in the *Asterix* comic series, a speaker not as optimistic as my humble self would say that we have come full circle in Africa.

Being an optimistic speaker means that I must hasten to conclude this part of our exercise on depression and pretend that the atavism of crisis and conflict is not part of the tableau of depression. I am therefore not going to say that Congo is still as Conradianly dark as ever; I am not going to mention Boko Haram and South Sudan. Throwing crises and conflict into the mix will only delay us from asking the inevitable question: is there anything about the condition of Africa and the disciplines through which we generate modes of hermeneutic inquiry into the said condition that allows us to map anything other than one gory trajectory from colonial trauma to postcolonial abjection—with ten steps backward making nonsense of every step forward in a linear course?

I am assuming we all know what the politically correct answer to this question is: yes, there is much to celebrate in Africa and about Africa. It is not all doom and gloom. Luckily for us, logic and political correctness are in happy agreement here. It is logically untenable to stabilize doom and gloom as the permanent condition of any human society. Even in the most perilous of times which led to the tragic loss of their two most important dignitaries, one to death by suicide and the other to insanity, Umuofia and Umuaro had moments of triumph not arrested by the circumambient doom and gloom as articulated by the great novelist, Chinua Achebe.

However, beyond this happy marriage of logic and political correctness lies nuance. If we agree that elation and celebration have as much *droit de cité* in the African story as depression, gloom, and doom, we must ask the questions: How exactly did elation come into this picture? What is its trajectory? What are its contents? How do we account for the politics of back and forth between depression and elation, and what does it portend for disciplinary engagements of Africa? Consider these scenarios. Jean-Francois Bayart closed the 1980s on a note of gloom by announcing in 1989 that the state in Africa was doomed to a metaphysics of corruption. In *The State in Africa: The Politics of the Belly* (1993), the African state and her political practices were effectively placed under the conceptual control of Opapala, the Yoruba deity of hunger and gourmandizing in whose domain lies the stomach.

Ten years later, in 1999, Patrick Chabal and Jean-Pascal Daloz appeared to take a different tack in *Africa Works: Disorder as Political Instrument*. On the surface, it looked like we were finally getting a break from the depressing Afro-pessimism of the politics of the belly. We were approaching the uplifting territory of elation. But, wait a minute, *Africa Works*—differently? Isn't rationalizing informal networks of human and political agency—with the attendant argument to exclude ethics and value judgements—another way of saying that the usual ways and practices of democracy and the social contract would never work because Africa is somehow not culturally and ontologically attuned to those structures and practices of modernity? Even with *Africa Works,* have we really moved beyond the paradigm of depression in 1999?

No, you haven't, replied *The Economist* one year later, famously ushering the continent into a new millennium with the now famous or infamous caption: "The

Hopeless Continent" (2000). Things moved very quickly from here. You will observe that between 1994 and the early years of the 2000s, something was brewing beneath all this veneer of depression and pessimism. Something home-grown. A discourse of vision and hope anchored in cultural, economic, and political renewal, bearing the traceries of Négritude, cultural nationalism, and Pan-Africanism. Welcome to the discourse of African Renaissance and its associated agendas. Thabo Mbeki and his associates screamed African Renaissance throughout the 1990s. They convened a conference in 1998, published a book, founded an African Renaissance Institute, and went about organizing instead of agonizing. They gained little or no traction outside of South Africa. In the North, everybody was interested in depression and pessimism on account of Africa. Any talk of renaissance referred to that period from the fourteenth to the seventeenth century in Europe and not whatever some upstarts thought it meant in twenty-first century Africa.

Then, just as Mbeki and all those on the African Renaissance train finally began to gain a solid hearing in academia and beyond, those who had crowded out their voices with depression and pessimism suddenly announced that they had had a road to Damascus moment. We were advised to move on to the other extreme of celebration and elation. They said that something much bigger than a renaissance was happening in Africa. They had no room for the semantic nuancing through which Chabal and Daloz were able to deodorize disorder and the informal as legitimate praxes of agency in Africa. We were no longer in for any backdoor announcements of hope. Go tell it on the mountain that Africa is rising, has risen. *The Economist* (2013) tried to outdo *Time* magazine (2012). Africa Rising! Aspiring Africa! The Hopeful Continent! One glossy cover after the other screamed: Africa Rising!

I believe that an audience such as this should be sufficiently familiar with the content and career of this narrative of elation, which brushed aside age-long narratives of depression like Achebe's proverbial wildfire in the harmattan. Everything that was negative and depressing about the continent suddenly became positive and uplifting. Diction and registers changed: hopelessness became hopefulness; despondency became opportunity. Numbers and statistics rained torrentially from every imaginable source, bearing mouth-watering good news of "growth," "sustainable development," "governance," "democracy," "human rights," "rural and infrastructural development," "gender gap," "poverty," "education," etc.

I am sure you can expand this list infinitely. After all, you know by rote what the talking points and the keywords are in those PowerPoint slides whenever men in black suits from the international capital and finance community, the international development community, the global NGO and activist community, world governance bodies and their continental appendages in Africa, as well as the institutional and disciplinary world of the social sciences, descend on any seminar room to talk about Africa Rising. To these keywords and faddish phrases, we must add the fact that Africa Rising also comprises an ideological investment in the future. What used to be called a problematic youth bulge when we were in the era of depression and pessimism is now said to represent the continent's greatest advantage. She has the greatest number of youths on earth, and who says youth says innovation. Africa Rising is, therefore, African Innovation on the rise.

What could possibly be wrong with this picture, some of you may wonder. After all, there is enough going on in the continent to bear out the new narratives of elation. There was the Arab Spring, South Africa is in BRICS, Nigeria is MINT, democracy is spreading. This may be true, but a lot is wrong with the politics and philosophy of elation. There is the question of the suspicious timing of the rise of the discourse of Africa Rising. One African scholar who has raised this question is the celebrated Nigerian political scientist Professor Bayo Olukoshi. I was on a panel with him early this year in Pretoria, and he wondered aloud why the narrative of Africa Rising emerged only when the narrative of African Renaissance had finally begun to gain global attention. "Why and how did Africa Rising outshine African Renaissance?" Olukoshi asked the audience and enjoined them to think about it. President Thabo Mbeki was in the room . . .

It may be true that the suspicious timing of the rise of Africa Rising did have something to do with the growing fortunes of African Renaissance, but I have since found other issues to worry about. One of these issues is the provenance of the discourse of Africa Rising. That this narrative appears to have been born here in the West is not a problem for me. After all, Négritude was born in Paris and Black Paris of the interwar years is a legitimate theoretical framework for me. The problem, for me, is precisely where in the West the loudest noise about Africa Rising is always coming from. Google is a good Ifa Oracle to consult in these matters. I am worried that a casual Google search of this term almost always brings up the May 2014 Africa Rising conference of the IMF as the first and most important hit. You click on that link, and you are welcomed by the inevitable face of Christine Lagarde welcoming you to the conceptual territory of Africa Rising in a podcast and speech. I have stated earlier that we know all the keywords by rote so it must be easy for you to imagine the content of Mrs. Lagarde's speech without even reading it.

Other Google hits will take you inevitably to *The Economist* and *Time* magazine and all kinds of neoliberal think-tank work on Africa Rising. If you are patient, you will finally encounter some African input midway scrolling down to the bottom of your screen. You'll encounter the Africa Rising Foundation set up by Ndaba and Kweku Mandela, and you'll encounter, ironically, a podcast by a deputy governor of Nigeria's Central Bank, Kingsley Moghalu, claiming that Africa hasn't risen yet. Now, I don't know about you but whenever a new narrative about Africa seems to be domiciled mainly in the market-driven mansion of neoliberalism, I tend to develop severe allergies. My migraines tend to worsen whenever I encounter the IMF, the World Bank, *The Economist,* and Africa in the same sentence.

I am saying that it is a problem for me that every time I google Africa Rising, Christine Lagarde is always the first to appear on the scene to welcome me and conduct a guided tour of the concept. You google African Renaissance, Cheikh Anta Diop, Thabo Mbeki's speech, and the African Renaissance monument in Senegal are likely to be your first hits. Then you google Africa Rising and the IMF and *The Economist* are your first hits. This brings back Bayo Olukoshi's query and worry: why and how did the narrative of Africa Rising emerge to overshadow and supplant the narrative of African Renaissance?

This question could be framed differently: For whom is the Africa in African Renaissance being reborn? For whom is the Africa in Africa Rising rising? I do not want to address the first question here. At any rate, you probably can guess how I would answer the African Renaissance part of the question. My answer to the second part of this question may also seem obvious. You'd be right to conclude that I believe that Africa is not really rising for the African—at least not yet. You'd be right to conclude that I believe that Africa is rising mainly and predominantly for those screaming Africa Rising in Bretton Woods and their accomplices in the commanding heights of the continent's politics and economics. This explains why the narrative of Africa Rising is always powered by an insidious thematic of rich pickings. Africa Rising would have no meaning beyond market orthodoxy and investment friendliness. Africa is rich pickings! Go ye hither and exploit all the opportunities before wily China laps up everything!

These obvious answers mask a deeper concern. Africa Rising invites us to take a closer look at the question of African agency. As one looks at the glass display cases of triumphalist and exultant neoliberalism, many African countries are on display: Ghana, Botswana, South Africa, Kenya, Namibia, etc. After every election meeting the minimal requirements of democracy, new countries are installed in new glass display cases and brandished to the world as the latest success stories from Africa. Yet, as you window-shop and look at these African countries glistening in display cases, your mind returns again and again to the question of agency. What was the African's role in the construction of these glass showcases and what say did he have in the politics of inhabiting that glass display case?

Let me illustrate this point with an anecdote. I was discussing Ghana at the beginning of this talk. I was lamenting the fact that the country is now in the final phase of negotiations with the IMF for a bailout loan because of "market-driven" shocks. I was lamenting the fact that Madame Christine Lagarde was talking enthusiastically about a new "policy mix" for Ghana by the IMF. We all know that this is all a honey-coated way of saying that Ghana has failed and is now back in Washington, cap in hand, begging for the loans that will predictably ruin the future of the next three generations of Ghanaians. The African Union has been talking about the Africa 2063 Agenda. I was involved with the Diaspora Consultations on this agenda in New York last year. It seems to me that the question of what Africa ought to look like in 2063 is already being settled in the case of Ghana. The year 2063 will meet Ghana repaying loans and renegotiating the terms and conditionalities of the policy mix being conjured today by Getafix Lagarde.

Yet, this is the only country in West Africa that was placed in a glass display case by Africa Rising for more than a decade. Much to the envy and annoyance of Ghana's eternal rival, Nigeria, the usual suspects in the choir of Africa Rising screamed from the rooftops that Ghana was the beacon of hope for the continent. All the usual ingredients of discourse flooded the global public sphere in relation to Ghana: political stability, growth, democracy, jobs, infrastructural expansion, etc. So, how did we get to being unable to pay salaries after ferrying three million dollars cash to football players in Brazil? How did we get to the perdition that are IMF loans and bailouts?

I spent a year in Ghana. I only just returned in the summer. On arrival in Ghana, I couldn't believe the level of development that I saw. Stable electricity and stable water from the taps: these two alone are enough to make a Nigerian award the Nobel Prize in Infrastructure to any country because they have not been part of our national experience since the early 1980s. Add to that the gleaming and glistening infrastructure that I saw all over the place and you would forgive me for taking enthusiastically to social media to declare that it was criminally unfair to place Ghana in the same third-world bracket as Nigeria and other less fortunate African countries where electricity and tap water are never regular. Yet, Ghana was not yet at the second-world level of South Africa. I decided to hang her in a no-man's land between the second and third worlds.

However, something made me perpetually uneasy about the infrastructure and modernity that I saw all around me in Ghana. I was only able to identify the source of my unease five months into my stay. It was the jeeps! There were way too many jeeps on the roads of Accra for my liking. No, I am not talking about private jeeps belonging to individuals. I am talking about what I call postcolonial jeepology, a phenomenon in which jeeps bring the symbolism of foreign aid and dependency to the doorsteps of the postcolony. You should be able to visualize those UN jeeps by now. I mean those white Toyota Prado jeeps that are so ubiquitous in Africa. They bear the insignia of every imaginable specialized agency of the United Nations: FAO, UNICEF, UNCHS, WHO, etc. The glut of white jeeps is not the singular making of the UN. The European Union, International Development Agencies, International Development Partners, all kinds of foundations, from Bill and Melinda Gates to Clinton, Christian missions and charity organizations—everybody is pumping jeeps and experts into Africa.

I was at the University of Ghana. The campus is crawling with the jeeps of postcolonial aid dependency. I visited ministries in town and other institutions of state—jeeps and jeeps everywhere. WHO-assisted this, IDRC-assisted that, European Union–assisted this, DANIDA-assisted that, German government–assisted this, French government–assisted that. Now, my own rule of thumb is that any African country crawling under the weight of the white jeeps of postcolonial dependency is in trouble. It means that the modernity you see all around you is contrived, fragile, and artificially propped by ways and means that do not belong to you. It means that somebody somewhere is desperate for a narrative, for a showpiece, and is pouring resources and symbols into a particular space to prop it up as that showpiece and produce a desired narrative.

These postcolonial white jeeps of dependency power a narrative of representation hoisted for the visual satisfaction of the giver. This is why President Obama went to Ghana. And the mirror beamed an African success story at him, and he sermonized to Africa from that location. This is Africa Rising, President Obama screamed. This is Ghana in which Washington is well pleased. We want y'all in the rest of the continent to be like her. Today, Obama's showpiece is at the IMF begging for loans. The IMF spent the '80s and the '90s producing those children with countable ribs and mucus-drenched nostrils with policies designed to guarantee starvation across the continent so long as the market was growing. Evidence of failure only yielded more prescriptions of the same policies and lectures that Africa was not applying them properly. Things got so bad that Nobel Prize–winning economist, Joseph Stiglitz had to draw the line for the West. Somebody somewhere desperately needed a narrative of success. Ghana was just the sort of candidate needed and ready for the assignment.

What this means is that there is little or no African agency in the modernity of the white Toyota Prado jeeps of postcolonial aid dependency. What would happen if these jeeps were suddenly withdrawn, I kept wondering in Accra. I got a taste of what could potentially happen in my last two months in the country. Power cuts made a rude intrusion into my life; water supply followed suit and became erratic; salaries started to be delayed; everybody groaned on campus and in town; the cedi plunged into a free fall. By the time I was leaving Accra in August, echoes of Ebola were rumbling in Guinea and Liberia, and we prayed for that cup to pass over Ghana. When your Africa Rising narrative is unravelling, when you are only just discovering for whom your Africa was really rising all this time you thought she was rising for you, you do not want Ebola to be the coup de grâce. Thankfully, Ebola spared Ghana.

What do these scenarios portend for you as graduate students and scholars of Africa? For starters, it means that the disciplinary space between elation and depression has not been fully probed in terms of our efforts to understand the dynamics of that continent. It means that we are yet to account for the elusiveness of agency and we do not even fully understand why it remains elusive and perpetually beyond grasp in Africa. If we do not understand why we lack agency, we will never find our way to it.

For instance, you'd think that almost four decades of writing back in and through the disciplines of the social sciences and humanities; of telling and retelling our story as Africans and Africanists as we see in Paul Zeleza's (2003) remarkable book, *Manufacturing African Studies and Crises;* of detailing and accounting for the significance of Africa to the disciplines as was done in the book, *Africa and the Disciplines* (Bates, O'Barr, & Mudimbe, 1993); you'd think that all these disciplinary gains and insights would have rendered us masters of our destiny in the field of representation. You'd think that we would have become more secure and stable owners of Africa's story by now, owning your story and the means of its narrativization being a precondition for agency. Yet, somehow, we never owned the Joseph Kony story, never owned #BringBackOurGirls, and do presently not own the framing of the narrative of Ebola. If a continent cannot even own the means to perspectivize her failures and her tragedies, how can she possibly own the path to her successes and triumphs?

My own field, African literature, falls prey to this play of agency in interesting ways. Where is agency located and enabled in terms of literature as a canonized institution? The recent social media spat between my friends, Kenyan author Binyavanga Wainaina and Nigerian thinker and literary "papa terrible," Ikhide Ikheloa (he is too old to be called an enfant terrible), is a good case in point. Binyavanga has been a relentless critic of the Caine Prize in recent times. If you want to be unkind, you'll say that our man Binya is kicking at the ladder he rode to literary stardom. He believes it is overrated and has acquired too much power in the canonization and validation of African literatures. He whines and whines and whines. It gets on Ikhide's nerves. Ikhide is angry that the Nigeria Prize for Literature, a US$100,000-prize awarded annually, is an annual ritual of literary powerlessness and oblivion.

A prize worth £15,000 is awarded to an African short story, and it comes with an international media buzz announcing instant canonization. One hundred thousand dollars is awarded to a writer in Nigeria, and he'd be lucky to be interviewed grudgingly by two or three local newspapers. Ikhide is mad as hell about this development. So he dismisses Binyavanga's endless whining about the Caine Prize. Stop complaining about the white man, he screams, go and develop and empower your own prizes and narratives in Africa! If you have no clue how to empower your own cultural and institutional modes of literary valuation in Africa, stop whining about the white man, Ikhide screams.

It should be obvious to those of you in literature that the interface between the Caine Prize and the Nigerian Prize for Literature offers grounds for interrogating agency, power, and modes of privileging in your field. If Africa is rising for the African, how does one account for the fact a literary prize worth $100,000 in Africa guarantees oblivion for an African writer and another prize worth less than half of that amount awarded in Europe guarantees instant superstardom, including paradoxically in Africa? How does one engage the seeming unwillingness to apply ourselves in Nigeria and in Africa to the task of empowering the Nigerian Prize for Literature?

One last area of disciplinary consequence I want to mention is the question of finding appropriate idioms for the persisting disjuncture and disconnect between reality and the etiquette of disciplinary narrativizing in the age of political correctness and anti-essentialism. This past year that I spent in Ghana came with the added advantage of extensive travels in the continent. Those who were loath to paying my way for lectures such as this because of the cost of flying me from Ottawa could suddenly afford to fly me from Accra. I crisscrossed the continent for lectures, but I was also a keen observer of the life and pulse of Africa. I saw gains. I saw pains. I saw evidence of Africa Rising but not with or for the African. About the only thing I saw rising is the hard-earned income of the poverty-stricken African rising into the pocket of his pastor as prosperity Pentecostalism rages across the continent to fill the vacuum abandoned by the state and her institutions.

In too many cases, Africa is simply rising without or beyond the African. Africa cannot really be said to be rising if the state still mainly demissions from the social contract and her gleaming institutions rise to satisfy the empirical and statistical parameters of outsiders at the expense of the peoples of Africa. Do the disciplines have a language for these confounding dynamics beyond the patronizing depression of Afro-pessimism? Where the idiom is lacking, do we focus on the evidence of progress which abounds and veer into unnuanced Afro-optimism?

Kofi Annan (2014) grumbled about the response of the international community to Ebola. Says Annan on the BBC:

> If the crisis had hit some other region it probably would have been handled very differently. In fact when you look at the evolution of the crisis, the international community really woke up when the disease got to America and Europe.

This is one of Africa's most famous and illustrious sons telling us that Africa has not risen. Europe and America ought to have moved in faster with white Toyota Prado jeeps to tackle Ebola. The day that Africa would be able to take care of business such as this without waiting to condemn Euro-America for not playing the traditional role of the savior quickly enough, Africa would truly have risen for the African.

I wish you successful deliberations in this conference.

Africa Is People, Nigeria Is Nigerians

Provocations on Post-mendicant Economies

guess it is in the character of my friend, Khalil Shariff, CEO of the Aga Khan Foundation Canada, to put one on a podium before a distinguished assemblage of guests comprised of members of the diplomatic community, members of Parliament, directors in the Canadian Foreign Affairs Ministry, staff of international development agencies, CEOs from corporate Canada, and senior academics, and ask one to get the discussion rolling with a ten-minute opening address! As if it wouldn't take the whole day to thank him, Rishma Thomas, Jennifer Pepall, and the wonderful staff of the Aga Khan Foundation Canada for the extraordinary honor of being asked to share my thoughts with you as one of two guests of honor for today's event!

As if it wouldn't take the whole day to thank the co-organizers of this event, the High Commission of the Republic of South Africa! How can I possibly thank my sister, Her Excellency Mohau Pheko, the high commissioner of South Africa in Canada, in just ten minutes? Her service here in Ottawa has been marked, among several remarkable firsts, by robust efforts to harness Africa's intellectual energies in the capital city. Although I carry a Nigerian passport and a Canadian passport,

Keynote Remarks at Aga Khan Foundation Canada's Parley, Monday, November 28, 2011.

her leadership and vision are such that I am regularly solicited to be part of an unending run of Africa-focused intellectual initiatives emanating from her table. If you feel Africa constantly vibrating intellectually here in Ottawa, you need not look beyond the leadership provided by the South African High Commission. I must add, though, that Her Excellency is a bad businesswoman! You see, the first rule of business is to discourage competition. The South Africans are very huge players in the Nigerian economy. She should keep that a secret from Canadian competition, no? Now she's given me an opportunity to tell all the Canadian CEOs present here to go to Nigeria and compete with the South Africans!

I must confess that the advertised theme of today's event, "Africa's Promise, Canada's Opportunity: A Conversation with Pius Adesanmi and David Creighton," unsettled me a bit. I could understand my fellow guest of honor, David Creighton, being at home in this environment. He is a powerful Canadian CEO whose empire is active in more than fifty countries in Africa and the rest of the developing world; he is a top player in Nigeria's Mouka Foam and Diamond Bank. That makes him a prime candidate for the hardware language of business and international investment. He is going to be able to break Africa down to figures and statistics and speak the language of investment opportunities, risks, returns, dividends, and profit. Where is the place for my software language of literature, culture, and the imagination in all this? When, for instance, I saw the name of the president and CEO of Bombardier on your guest list, I wondered if it wouldn't be more appropriate to have Nigerian state governors, prosperity Pentecostal pastors, or even President Jonathan, who keeps a harem of presidential jets and feels morally obliged to buy new ones every now and then, address him instead of a poor teacher like me.

Rishma allayed my fears during our telephone conversations in the build-up to this event. I saw a lot of sense in the fact that the organizers wanted my own historical-culturalist perspective to serve as context for David Creighton's statistical and empirical CEO-speak. I took solace in the fact that Chinua Achebe, long before me, also had the same experience in Paris. In his essay, "Africa Is People"–now you know where my title comes from!—Achebe narrates his bewilderment at being invited to address a parley of the Organization for Economic Corporation and Development (OECD). Let's listen to Achebe (1999) in some detail:

> I believe it was in the first weeks of 1989 that I received an invitation to an anniversary meeting—the twenty-fifth year, or something like that—of the Organization for Economic Cooperation and Development (OECD) in Paris. I accepted without

quite figuring out what I could possibly contribute to such a meeting/celebration. My initial puzzlement continued right into the meeting itself. In fact, it grew as the proceedings got under way. Here was I, an African novelist among predominantly European and American bankers and economists; a guest, as it were, from the world's poverty-stricken provinces to a gathering of the rich and powerful in the metropolis. As I listened to them—Europeans, Americans, Canadians, Australians—I was left in no doubt by the assurance they displayed that these were the masters of our world savoring the benefits of their success. They read and discussed papers on economic and development matters in different regions of the world. They talked in particular about the magic bullet of the 1980s, structural adjustment, specially designed for those parts of the world where economies had gone completely haywire. The matter was really simple, the experts seemed to be saying; the only reason for failure to develop was indiscipline of all kinds, and the remedy was a quick, sharp administration of shock treatment that would yank the sufferer out of the swamp of improvidence back onto the high and firm road of free-market economy.

Achebe could have been describing you, my audience here today! Almost ten years later, in 1998, Achebe delivered a Presidential Fellows Lecture at the World Bank in Washington and expressed pretty much the same apprehension. On both occasions, my famous compatriot appealed to "the masters of our world" to think of Africa as people and not just resources and the promise of profit, hence his topic, "Africa is People." Since you have asked David and me to lay out broad parameters and provocations that would guide our day-long conversations and interactions in the morning and evening schedules of this event, my first provocation of the day is to ask you to seriously consider Achebe's plea to the OECD and the World Bank. I know that you are precisely the kind of actors that African states have in mind—especially Nigeria—when they mouth the endless rhetoric of Foreign Direct Investment (FDI). I know that you have been invited here to listen to new insights about where resources and profit abound in Africa and how to reach those in the context of new global dynamics. But I say to you that there needs to be a shift from the paradigm that always privileges Africa (resources) over Africans (people). If the model of Africa before Africans worked, we wouldn't be here today essaying a rethink, would we?

When I ask you to think of Africa as people, I am not asking you to see one billion people and immediately begin to dream of a market that now rivals the economies of the BRIC and the Asian Tigers and is even now more positively discoursed in global geopolitics than those two players are. Therein lies my second provocation of the day: if Africa is people, she is also history and culture. You cannot get at our resources by ignoring those two elements. When you try it, there are guys out there in the field waiting to teach you that their history and culture constitute who they are, and who they are is more important than copper, crude oil, and coltan. Go and study Ken Saro-Wiwa's rhetoric and praxis.

So, what is the history of this one billion people? How have we arrived at a situation where that talented one billion is now whetting appetites here in the West as the market of the present and the future? Well, you must understand that they moved from four centuries of the transatlantic slave trade to one momentous century that my friend, Okwui Enwezor (2001), has famously described as "the short century." The short century extends from the Berlin conference in 1884 to the independence of South Africa in 1994. In other words, it is the century of colonialism. At the end of all these experiences, this one billion people became humanity's byword for poverty, disease, famine, malnutrition, civil wars, corruption, illiteracy, and a million other registers of negativity and underdevelopment that are trafficked ceaselessly by the Western media. In May 2000, the verdict on Africa came in: "The Hopeless Continent" screamed *The Economist* in a famous edition of the magazine.

Fast-forward to 2010 and we arrive at my third provocation. The McKinsey Global Institute (2010) released its famous report on Africa entitled, "Lions on the Move: The Progress and Potential of African Economies." I implore you to google and read that rigorously researched and exhilarating report. Its eighty-two pages brim with sweet music for the ears of an African public intellectual like me. What detains me here, though, is the cognitive and descriptive shift of the report: African Lions versus Asian Tigers! How did we move from a summation of Africa as a "hopeless continent" in 2000 to a situation where we now speak of viable "economic lions" that would have surpassed the BRIC and the Asian Tigers by 2040? What happened in just ten years in Africa? That is something I want us to ponder seriously as we get down to business today.

However, we should not discuss the rise of what I call Africa's post-mendicant economies in a vacuum. Here, I am almost tempted to gloat! We should discuss Africa against the background of what is happening on the economic front in your own home continent: Europe. Fate and irony have a way of playing funny games. The continent that enslaved and colonized us, the continent that proceeded to describe us as the hopeless antithesis to civilization and modernity, is now home to the world's mendicant economies. From Greece to Britain via Italy and Ireland, the specter of a beggarly Europe cannot be divorced from the specter of a rising Africa, what with prosperous Angola now even considering giving financial aid prostrate Portugal. Ah, life! One must however warn our brothers in Angola to learn from the tragedy of Nigeria, whose charity always begins abroad, before shipping bucket loads of dollars to aid poor Portugal.

But I ask again: how did Africa achieve this extraordinary reversal of fortunes? Specialists speak of the expansion and consolidation of democratic ethos across the continent. From South Africa to Ghana, Botswana to Zambia, Rwanda to Benin Republic, elections and other signposts of democracy are getting better, never mind the persistence of election basket cases like Nigeria, Zimbabwe, and Uganda. Other factors suggested for the rise of Africa as a global economic player include the emergence of a vibrant civil society, the rise of the African middle class, and the expansion of options of international competition and viability with China and Brazil becoming major players in the continent's economies. I have no problems with all these explanations proposed by relevant literature, but I want us to reflect further particularly on just one—the middle class.

I do not want to bore you with a rehash of the historical role of the middle classes in the rise of the modern nation-state. It is history too well known. Suffice it to say that one of the tragedies of postcolonial Africa is precisely the systematic destruction of that class in the period known as post-independence disillusionment. My own country bears testimony to this tragedy. The military, especially, Ibrahim Babangida, destroyed Nigeria's middle class. The highpoint of the destruction of Africa's middle class also coincides with the era of the wholesale application of the moronic prescriptions of the IMF and the World Bank. The structural adjustment programs prescribed by your people really ruined us in Africa.

Today, we speak of a billion people. We say that sixty-five percent of that billion people is under the age of forty-five. Some figures even put it at thirty-five! That's a lot of people in a very youthful middleclass. They are the ones who have risen from the ashes of structural adjustment to build the Africa that we encounter in the McKinsey report. They are educated, urbanized, resourceful, adventurous, and very cosmopolitan. In Nigeria, they wield two or three BlackBerries per head. They are all over Facebook and Twitter. They are changing the modes and content of urbanization in Africa. In a number of cases, they are even in charge of the state. Their tastes and cultural habits represent the opportunities that you, Canadian investors, are going to meet on the ground in Africa. But it should be clear from my submissions thus far that you cannot go and engage them on the terms of yesterday.

I must end these provocations by saying that a huge chunk of this vibrant African middle class is domiciled in Nigeria. We've got the population, and we tend to remind people of it as a mark of our importance. You will also have noticed my reluctance to talk about Nigeria when talking about the positive indices from the continent. That is due to my low opinion of the political class in Nigeria. I hold the rulers of Nigeria in utter contempt. They are corrupt and intellectually inferior. They run a moribund state. They have nothing to offer Nigerians and the rest of the world. In my own intellectual praxis, I consider Nigeria a case of 160 million good people strangely held hostage by the worst characters among them. If you are looking for an example of their intellectual impecuniosity, think of President Goodluck Jonathan's proposed solution to the security challenge posed by Boko Haram: ignore it! Yes, you heard me right. You just go into Nigeria, invest your billions, ignore Boko Haram, and every other thing shall be added unto you.

My challenge here, as we go on to discuss and reflect on issues after David's opening remarks, will be to get you to look beyond these characters and see the Nigerian people. If Africa is people, Nigeria is Nigerians. And the reality on the ground is that the contribution of the Nigerian people, especially the Nigerian middle class, to Africa's economic rebirth, has happened in spite of and not because of the Nigerian state. Despite insecurity, despite corruption, despite unimaginative rulership, there is no speaking of Africa's promise without the Nigerian people. You are going to have to cut through the challenges to deal with us because all 160 million of us are a people before we are a market. I look forward to fruitful deliberations for the rest of the day.

The Disappeared African Roots
of Emma Watson's UN Feminism

Feminism stole the show at the recently concluded UN General Assembly in New York. If by now you have not heard that actress Emma Watson delivered a feminist speech, which became the most celebrated event during that week of frenzied activities at the UN, you must have taken a short vacation from human civilization to reside in a cave. Emma Watson's (2014) feminist speech is everywhere, its fame rivalled perhaps only by #BringBackOurGirls and the Joseph Kony campaign before it.

Facebook trended the speech like the second coming of Jesus Christ. Twitter told it on the mountain, over the hills and everywhere that Emma Watson had taken feminism to heights no one had ever imagined. Not to be outdone, *Vanity Fair* called it "a game-changing speech on feminism" (Robinson, 2014). The feminist establishment, activist and academic, went gaga, especially here in North America. The usual construction, deconstruction, and reconstruction of the speech started; rethinking of it started; remapping of it started. I followed the rise to fame and incipient theoretical career of the speech with considerable bemusement and amusement. You will know why shortly.

I was going to brush the speech aside and return to my daily political preoccupation with the Nigerian tragedy when I received an enthusiastic email from a

Nigerian graduate student in the United States. "Prof, have you read Emma Watson's UN speech? Fantastic, isn't it? Are you planning to come to the ALA next year? I was thinking we could convene a panel on it. We could examine the theoretical implications of the speech for African feminist discourse." The ALA, for the reader not in academia, is the African Literature Association, the annual mecca of those of us in the business of producing knowledges on the literatures of Africa.

This is the point at which I decide that Emma Watson's UN speech has become Chinua Achebe's proverbial leper. Allow him a handshake and he will insist on a bear hug the next time. It is one thing for me to watch, bemused and amused, as the West canonized and proclaimed the speech as the most original line of thinking to have happened in feminism since Simone de Beauvoir discovered in 1949 that one is not born a woman but rather becomes a woman; it is another thing to hear an African drool over its originality, proposing to take it to the ALA to start a new line of thinking in African feminisms.

I have spent almost two decades in the universities of the United States and Canada. I am used to the West constantly proclaiming the originality of some new proposition in the arena of knowledge largely because Western canonizers of knowledge are very much like the child in that Yoruba proverb who, never having visited other people's farms, screams from the rooftop that his father owns the biggest farm in the world. You go to the disciplines of the humanities and you see people proclaiming the originality of some idea or philosophy that you heard unlettered farmers espouse every evening over palm wine in your village in Africa when you were growing up. If the West is hearing about it for the first time from a Western source, it is original.

So, what is the gist of this "original" speech by Emma Watson that has gotten everybody so excited? Ms. Watson says that she has had a road to Damascus moment in the entire business of feminism. She has discovered from recent research that the word "feminist" is unpopular because of the prevalent notion that feminists are men-haters and male-bashers. She does not believe that the Boko Haramic men-bashing strategies of the most radical strands of feminism are helpful. She decries the anti-men, gender-war mongering of radical feminism which she claims alienates men and yields little results. Says Watson:

> In 1995, Hillary Clinton made a famous speech in Beijing about women's rights. Sadly many of the things she wanted to change are still a reality today. But what stood out for me the most was that only 30 percent of her audience were male. How

can we affect change in the world when only half of it is invited or feel welcome to participate in the conversation?

Consequently, she proposes a feminism of negotiation, of cooperation, of accommodation, of collaboration, of gender complementarity, of inclusion, which could make all us, men and women, feminists on the one hand while being sympathetic to issues of gender oppression that men also experience on the other hand. Hear her:

> Men—I would like to take this opportunity to extend your formal invitation. Gender equality is your issue too. Because to date, I've seen my father's role as a parent being valued less by society despite my needing his presence as a child as much as my mother's.

Stop bashing men. Include them. Make feminists of them. Gender equality ought to be everybody's business. Let's all do "HeForShe." That is the gist of Emma Watson's speech. That is what folks are saying they have never heard before. Well, I have. When feminist theory made it to Africa, it ran into troubled waters very quickly with African men and women alike. At the initial phase, Africa had the misfortune of encountering only the most radical strands of Western feminism. This feminism oozed smoke and fire from the center of its head like one of Fagunwa's ghomids. It was a very fearful feminism indeed. It tore at everything in Africa and lumped everything together: marriage and motherhood were just as bad as female genital surgery.

No African cultural and traditional institution passed muster. This rampaging radical Western feminism looked at the African woman, shook its head in pity, and declared her the most abject, the most oppressed human being it had ever encountered. It then declared that the white Western feminist savior had landed to rescue African women from their barbaric pagan men and patriarchal institutions. Naturally, this white feminist savior assumed that the way she experienced gender in her culture was universal.

African men panicked and began to blackmail African women who, it must be said, were sympathetic to feminisms. It became dangerous to be labeled a feminist. The tag came to carry all sorts of pejorative meanings. African women, especially the thinkers, recognized the problem of patriarchy and gender inequality in Africa. But they could not see themselves in the agendas and experiences of the white

Western radical feminist rampager who had come to save them from marriage, from motherhood, from men. They could not pretend that there were not elements of feminism in traditional Africa which were all thrown overboard by colonialism. After all, gender roles in traditional Africa did not always automatically translate to gender inequality. That I cultivated yams as a man and you dyed indigo for sale in the market as a woman does not intrinsically elevate male farmerhood over female traderhood. Also, African women thinkers could not overlook race—and so many other things.

Thus began the march to alternative ways of producing knowledges on the condition of African women, alternative ways of shedding light on African patriarchal issues, ways of saying that the experience of the white woman in Manhattan cannot be made to speak for the experience of the black woman in Mokola, Ibadan. This is the birth of African feminist discourses and action. Radical Western feminism cast such an alarming shadow over the emerging feminist discourses of Africa that some important African female writers even rushed to distance themselves from it. Ama Ata Aidoo (1986) of Ghana lashed out, "Feminism. You know how we feel about that embarrassing Western philosophy? The destroyer of homes. Imported mainly from America to ruin nice African homes." Nigeria's Buchi Emecheta (1988) was milder in her rejection of the feminist tag. She declared herself "a feminist with a small f."

So long as feminism was going to be a radical rampager from the West, the hesitation to embrace it would continue. Three Nigerians found a way out of the epistemological logjam. Eminent writer and feminist thinker, Molara Ogundipe-Leslie (1994), coined the term STIWANISM as a way of elaborating an African feminist theory and praxis that would not be open to the charges levelled against radical Western feminism and its intrusion into Africa. STIWA is her acronym for Social Transformation Including Women in Africa. In other words, she was proposing a feminism of cooperation and collaboration which does not bash or antagonize men. She was proposing a feminism which recognizes the complementarity of the two genders while not papering over the real issues affecting women in Africa.

She was not alone. Professor Obioma Nnaemeka, a mentor of mine, is arguably Nigeria's biggest contribution to contemporary feminist thought and critique on the world stage. She it was who came up with another theoretical category called NEGO-FEMINISM. Aunty Obioma was playing on words: "negotiated feminism and no ego feminism." (Nnaemeka, 1995). Nego-feminism also allowed for a praxis of complementarity and inclusion. In fact, she did not spare the rod in the canonical essay in which she introduced this new concept. She went after Western feminists who constantly misread Flora Nwapa, Chinua Achebe, and other African writers.

The late Catherine Acholonu (1995) completed this theoretical troika of African feminisms by suggesting the notion of MOTHERISM. In fact, Acholonu labeled motherism "an Afrocentric alternative to feminism." She had had enough of the demonization of motherhood in certain radical strands of Western feminism. Motherhood in Africa is a position of strength from which a feminist politics could be articulated. Like STIWANISM and NEGOFEMINISM, MOTHERISM is also a feminism of cooperation, collaboration, and inclusion.

Molara Ogundipe-Leslie's book was published in 1994. Catherine Acholonu's book was published in 1995. Obioma Nnaemeka also coined nego-feminism circa 1995. But all three thinkers had been discussing these issues long before the 1990s. Stiwanism, nego-feminism, and motherism are not just feminisms of HeForShe, they are also feminisms of SheForHe in conformity with the gender complementarity cultural bases of Africa.

African feminist theorists have been writing about these things for decades. They have proclaimed feminisms of inclusion from the podiums of the West since the 1980s. They have published books about these things in Western presses. Yet, folks are salivating over Emma Watson's speech as if they are hearing these things for the first time.

Perhaps this all boils down to Chinua Achebe's old argument about the necessity of telling our stories in order to achieve a balance of stories. All over Canada, all over the United States, graduate seminar syllabi on feminist theory will be designed subsequently to include "emergent HeForShe" feminist discourses. Students are going to be sent out to hunt for Emma Watson's speech as the source of this paradigm shift by professors for whom feminist theory does not extend beyond Simone de Beauvoir, Julia Kristeva, Helene Cixous, Luce Irigaray, Judith Butler, Betty Friedan, Toril Moi, Elaine Showalter, and Diana Fuss. If we do not tell our stories, nobody will remember that "HeForShe and SheForHe" feminism is not new. Nobody will remember that the Nigerian thinkers discussed here and their colleagues all over Africa have been screaming this feminism that the West is surprisingly only just discovering via Emma Watson for decades. The invitation extended to men by the actress was extended by African feminisms to men in the 1980s and 1990s. It remains an open invitation.

The Facebook and Twitter career of Emma Watson's speech has been aided by hundreds of thousands of young African netizens who have been sharing it enthusiastically with the obligatory rider about how original and refreshing it is. These kids, especially the Nigerians among them, have never heard of Obioma Nnaemeka, Molara Ogundipe-Leslie, and Catherine Acholonu. They do not know that what they are attributing to a British actress on a UN podium in New York are ideas patented about the time they were being born in the 1980s and 1990s by three great Nigerian feminist theorists. And that, my friends, is part of the tragedy of Africa.

The Africa Just Outside of Your Hilton Hotel Window

This is my third Black History Month event this year. More precisely, the third in which I am having to speak. I've attended nearly a dozen others as a cheering member of the audience. One theme seems to stand out this year, an overwhelming awareness of the urgency of owning and telling our stories: our stories as Black people, our stories as Africa people. That was the mandate given to me, for instance, by the African and Caribbean Students Union at McGill University, when I addressed their own Black History Month event a few weeks ago in Montreal.

The sentiment that Black humanity has stories to tell which are either silenced or improperly narrated, or narrated by others more powerful than us and for ends that have little to do with us, has been around since the beginning of modern Black imagination and intellectual thought. Many of the African and Black radical ideologies of the twentieth century were, in a very basic sense, efforts by Black people and Africans to attain what Chinua Achebe calls a "balance of stories."

No African or Black person needs to be introduced to the concrete consequences

Keynote lecture delivered at the Black History Month celebration of the African and Caribbean Students Union of St. Paul's University, Ottawa, February 26, 2016.

of our inability to own and tell our own stories. But not all of us understand that our reality, what shapes and informs our struggles here in the Western world, in the Caribbean, and on the mother continent Africa, is a function of stories and our ability to open up spaces of agency with stories. I will give you two examples to illustrate what I mean.

I arrived in Canada in the summer of 1998 to start my doctoral program at the University of British Columbia. A handful of us, Africans, had been admitted into various PhD programs across campus that year and we met and bonded as might be expected. My own immediate circle of African friends comprised two other Nigerian men and a Cameroonian lady, who happened to be the only one among us who lived in campus residence. The rest of us rented apartments in town.

I must mention that the Cameroonian lady in question is an Anglophone. Anglophone Cameroonians had been part of Nigeria before colonial mapping and remapping eventually dumped them in Cameroon as one Anglophone minority fish in a massive Francophone sea. In essence, Anglophone Cameroonians still share considerable cultural commonalities with the peoples of Nigeria's deep south, especially cuisine.

Our Cameroonian colleague was a great cook. Her residential apartment on campus became a regular stop for those of us who were lazy bachelors in the community of African doctoral students. She was constantly treating us to jollof rice, fufu, egusi, ogbono, efo riro, groundnut soup—spiced with all the ingredients of Africa.

Our culinary treats in her apartment lasted only a few weeks before trouble started. Her graduate student residential apartment was a three-bedroom affair with common areas: three students shared a living room, a kitchen, and two bathrooms. She was the only African in that set up. She had two Canadian roommates. One evening, I stopped by her apartment hoping to be treated to fufu and ogbono soup as usual but she offered to microwave a slice of pizza for me instead. You can imagine the disaster!

Then came her shocking story. She had been summoned by university residence administration because they received complaints from her roommates about the odor and the smell of her constant African cooking. She was advised to somehow tone down the smell of her food or cook in such a way as not to inconvenience her roommates.

"And what did you do?" I asked her.

"What can I do?" She asked in return, demonstrating her African cred, for only Africans answer questions with questions.

I assured her that there was plenty we could do. I assured her that there was plenty we needed to do. I wanted to know, for starters, if her roommates, those whose civilized nostrils had been offended by the foul odor and smell of African food, did any cooking of their own in the shared kitchen. Yes, they did. They cooked pasta. They baked quiche, tarts, and pizza. They made the obligatory poutine. And there was cheese in the fridge.

Armed with this information, we booked an appointment with university residence. When we got there, I had a few questions for them. I wanted them to explain to me how they arrived at the determination that Canadian cuisine had an aroma while African cuisine had an odor. I wanted them to explain to me how they arrived at a ranking of the smell of food which had Western food smelling really nice and African food oozing stench. I also wanted them to explain to me why they assumed that the African occupant of that apartment was not just as unadapted to the smell of the cooking of her Canadian roommates as they were to hers.

To cut a long story short, my Cameroonian friend earned the right to cook African delicacies again in her apartment because we insisted on telling stories. We recognized the fact that even in the business of gourmandizing, there are power relations and the difference between your food having an aroma or an odor could come down to your ability to tell your story efficiently.

What I want you to take away from this anecdote is the fact that a certain effort is put into telling your story in a certain kind of way. The conclusion that African food has odor and not aroma and the consequent "advice" to tone it down or do something about that odor is a function of a long chain of bureaucratic efforts.

The challenge, therefore, is not in always screaming that we are victims of misrepresentation, of stereotypes, of single stories. The point is: do you understand the fact that misrepresentations and stereotypes are products of effort and energy? Does your effort to tell your own story match the effort that is put into misrepresenting and stereotyping you?

Let us attempt a genealogy of the path to reductionist stereotypes and the considerable efforts involved. I have written elsewhere about a category of Western narrators of Africa I refer to as "the Hilton Hotel Africanist." This is the journalist or writer or scholar or documentary maker or adventurist or charity worker or development worker or expert or expatriate who arrives in any of the capital cities of the African continent, checks into the Hilton in town, and gets to work.

Getting to work means getting organized so that, eventually, our Africanist will be able to start sending dispatches back to the *New York Times* or the *Globe and Mail* or CNN or *Washington Post* and all that jazz. However, if you have been to the Hilton in any African capital, these hotels are always located in very posh and swanky areas of town. When our Africanist wakes up in the morning and opens his Hilton hotel window, the view of Africa which greets him is malls and skyscrapers and fast-moving luxury cars on glossy roads, telling stories of hypermodernity. The "Africans" he has met thus far in this setting are way beyond his pay grade. They can employ him very easily.

Yet, when he sends his dispatches about Africa back to Europe or America, nothing of this Africa he sees from his Hilton hotel window is present in the report. All that is left is Ebola, AIDS, Boko Haram, wars and conflict, hunger and malnutrition. All that is left are malnourished and naked children with eczema-ridden skin, mucus-filled noses studying under a tree using wooden slates donated by UNICEF.

How does this happen? It means that from his base in the Hilton hotel, this Africanist organizes expeditions into the Africa he has come to look for, hiring local agents to take him to locations of poverty and despair, completely ignoring the modernity to which he returns in the capital every evening.

In essence, it takes a lot of effort to produce a documentary reducing you to Ebola; it takes a lot of organization to send a dispatch back to New York or London, reducing more than a billion people in fifty-four countries to hunger and malnutrition. It takes exceptional willpower and effort to close your mind and consciousness to all the postmodern gloss you see around you in the neighborhood of your Hilton hotel in Abuja or Nairobi or Johannesburg just because you are fixated on making poverty porn for consumption by Western audiences.

It takes effort and considerable organization and diligence to tell lies about you or distort your story. Once your story is distorted, your world is equally distorted. Does Africa understand that it also takes effort and organization and dedication to tell your own truths? I think somebody in Africa understands this better than we do: China. Many of you here are perhaps already aware of the fact that there is a story called China in Africa. This has been the dominant story out of Africa for nearly a decade. Everybody is talking about China in Africa.

The West has also been doing a lot of talking about China in Africa. And the West has been saying that the sky is falling. All the usual spokespersons of the West have been demonizing China. As secretary of state, Hillary Clinton once toured Africa to warn us about the dangers of China. Of course we know that the West is not sensitizing us to the dangers of dalliance with China because she loves Africa so much. It is the fear of competition and displeasure at being overtaken by China in the scramble for the resources of Africa that is determining the way in which the West is shaping the story of China in Africa.

What did China do? Well, somebody in Beijing apparently decided that they were not going to let the West tell their story in Africa. They decided that they would not let the idea of China in Africa be shaped exclusively by CNN, BBC, France 24, the *New York Times,* and the *Washington Post.* They invested heavily in CCTV Africa, China's answer to the West's global cable television machine. CCTV Africa is heavily subsidized by China. It is as popular as Al Jazeera in the continent. Yet, the sole ideological function of that television is to enable China to tell her own story in Africa.

Moral of this story: the future belongs to those who understand the fact that efforts to reduce you to a story must be matched or overwhelmed by your own efforts to shine as a diversity of stories.

That is the challenge before Black people.

That is the challenge before Africa.

I thank you for your time!

PART TWO

Imagining Culture, Figuring Change

Capitalism and Memory

Of Golf Courses and Massage Parlors in Badagry, Nigeria

Sarah Quesada's invitation letter stated that this conference is convened jointly by the Stanford Forum for African Studies (SFAS), the Stanford Division of Languages, Cultures, and Literatures, and the Center for African Studies. I want to thank all three units for the extraordinary privilege of being asked to mount a Stanford podium and deliver a keynote lecture at a time when Stanford University and keynote lectures have become the new cool online thanks to the life and genius of one of America's greatest gifts to humanity: Steve Jobs.

Because he is no longer with us and precisely because my reference to his commencement address here at Stanford University in 2005, and the modes of its preservation, canonization, and dissemination online, evoke modes of remembering and the ritual of totemizing the remembered by collapsing the distance between the profane and the sacred, I cannot but see in the evocation of that illustrious Stanford commencement speaker a segue to the keyword around which I am going to organize my thoughts in this lecture: memory.

Keynote lecture delivered at the annual conference of the Stanford Forum for African Studies, Palo Alto, California, Saturday, October 29, 2011

Bearing this in mind let me first acknowledge obvious debts of intellectual and theoretical filiation. My title, "Capitalism and Memory," speaks of a direct debt to Eric Williams's (1944) magnum opus, *Capitalism and Slavery,* just as the theme you have chosen for your conference, "The Black Atlantic: Colonial and Contemporary Exchanges," speaks of your conceptual debt to Paul Gilroy (1993) and the cottage industry of theoretical disquisition spawned by his brilliant book, *The Black Atlantic.* At a slightly different remove from these two classics are two other monumentally important books that are equally going to haunt my submissions here: Walter Rodney's (1983) *How Europe Underdeveloped Africa* and Eduardo Galeano's (1973) *Open Veins of Latin America.* The echoes of each work will, hopefully, be loud enough for you not to miss them as I proceed with my current effort cautiously in the shadow of what has come before it. "Iba—For Those Who Went Before," says Wole Soyinka in a Yoruba reiterative act of acknowledging the superiority of precedence.[1]

The difference between my project and what obtains in the epistemic field of these illustrious precursors is one of slant and nuance. Eric Williams's economism, for instance, remains one of the most powerful and moving accounts of how the symbolic elements that David Diop (1974) builds into one of the most famous bursts of imagery in African poetry, "the blood of your sweat/the sweat of your work/the work of your slavery/the slavery of your children," are all to be found at the foundation of capitalism. Blood. Sweat. Work: the foundation of mercantilist capitalism, industrial capitalism, colonialist capitalism, and all their heirs and hues in our postmodern present when corporate capitalism and casino capitalism (apologies to Susan Strange) are now pretending that we shall forget the paths they traveled and their bloody history once they rename themselves globalization.

Those of you who have read Eric Williams (1944) attentively would have noticed that he refers to the energies which capitalism hunted, captured, transported, organized, brutalized, and exploited in the historical process of its own self-constitution and the deification of profit as events whose unfolding could be mapped into linear and specific temporalities. In fact, in chapter 8, entitled "The New Industrial Order," Williams mentions "three events" whose abolition is "inseparable" in terms of consequences: slavery, the slave trade, and the sugar preference of the West Indian monopoly capitalists. If you look at the other texts by Eduardo Galeano and Walter Rodney that I mentioned earlier, the narrative of capitalism also essentially comes

---

1. The "Iba" reference is drawn from Soyinka's memoir, *You Must Set Forth at Dawn.*

down to specific events authored by the capitalist West on the backs of the peoples of Africa and Latin America.

However, I am interested in something much deeper and more abstract than the physicality of these events. I am trying to look beyond the specific ways in which capitalism, be it of the mercantilist, industrialist, corporatist, or casino ilk, has organized human history and experience for five centuries as one grand biography of the beast called profit. To look beyond the physicality of the events in question is to move into the abstract territory of the sacred where we encounter the memory of things experienced. Emile Durkheim always comes into the picture whenever I am summoned to reflect on the ways in which Africa and her Diaspora have negotiated the memory of things done to them by capitalism on the one hand and the ways in which they have transformed that memory into a space of contact and engagements, which often acquire the halo of the sacred, on the other hand.

Privileging an abstraction such as memory over the physicality of the event of slavery itself allows me to work around some of the aporias and fissures associated with the theory of Paul Gilroy and the dramaturgy of, say, August Wilson in terms of where to locate and map the contact zones between Africa and her Diaspora. The narrative of black trauma begins *in medias res* with Gilroy (1993) in *The Black Atlantic,* what with his emphasis on the image of the Atlantic Ocean and the slave ship gliding on it, both serving as the historical crucible for "the structures of feeling, producing, communicating, and remembering" (p. 3) that Gilroy names "the black Atlantic world." One obvious problem with a project that traces the roots and routes of these things to the Middle Passage and not to Africa per se is the ease with which we resituate Europe as the History in our histories while ironically claiming to be deconstructing Europe, provincializing Europe, or moving the center. Hence, what detains Gilroy in chapters 4 and 5 of his book is the route that led W. E. B Du Bois to Germany and Richard Wright to France. Ghana, such a monumentally important destination for the two men, is thrown sparingly into the picture.

For all the echoes of Africa in the dramaturgy of August Wilson, it is difficult to overlook the fact that the roots and routes of black historical trauma head more in the direction of the Middle Passage than Africa. The floor of the Atlantic Ocean appears to be the beginning of things. Like William Faulkner's Yoknapatawpha County, Wilson creates his own fictional world, the mythical City of Bones on the floor of the Atlantic Ocean, where the bones of all the slaves thrown overboard become source and origin. Hence, Harry J. Elam Jr. (2009) is able to describe the City of Bones as "a site that reunites or re-members the collective black body, those lost old bones, making them into a unified structure, a communal site. It is a city that joins past to present and that overcomes loss by recuperating and dynamically maintaining a living African American history" (p. 236). This explains why it is not too difficult for any native Yoruba to gauge the extraordinary leaps and stretches that Elam has to perform in order to locate Ogun, via Soyinka, as the backcloth of August Wilson's dramaturgy.

The considerably reduced enunciation of Africa in these approaches to narratives of blackness and black trauma is perhaps indicative of much deeper fissures in the black body politic, which underscore the necessity of reconfiguring memory and its fractal sites of actuation in Africa and the Diaspora. Evidence of such fissures abounds on both sides—in Africa and the Diaspora. Consider the long history of return narratives, the memories they bear, and the imaginaries they perform. The return narrative is a gigantic cultural genre with numerous strands. There is the spiritual-mythic return of *Le vieux* Médouze whose soul returns to Guinée after his transition to ancestorhood in Euzhan Palcy's great film, *Sugar Cane Alley;* there is the radical, reverse-exodus model of Marcus Garvey. The eulogistic Négritude model of the Aimé Césaire of the "eias," the fundamentalist nativism of the Léon Damas of the "poupées noires" fame; the ambivalence of the Richard Wright of *Black Power;* the blame-Africans-for-slavery-and-exculpate-the-white-slaver proclivities of Henry Louis Gates Jr.; and the I-am-washing-my-hands-of-that-miserable-and-better-forgotten-continent, Pontius Pilate approach of Keith Richburg are all divergent strands of the grand epic that is the return narrative.

As disparate as they are, something unites these various models of the return narrative: the anxiety of contact, the initial fear of the unknown that houses your origin. This anxiety is captured most vividly in the opening page of Richard Wright's (1954) *Black Power:* "Now that your desk is clear, why don't you go to Africa," Dorothy Padmore tells Mr. Wright. "*Africa?*" Mr. Wright's dumbfoundment is italicized in the text. Then this bit of introspection: "'Africa,' I repeated the word to myself, (n.b., Africa is still only a word) then paused as something strange and disturbing stirred slowly in the depths of me. I am African! I'm of African descent . . . Yet I'd never seen Africa; I'd never really known any Africans; I'd hardly ever thought of Africa." The entire opening section of *Black Power* is a paean to the anxiety of contact.

What I call the anxiety of contact as the unifying dialect of return narratives, no matter how disparate they are, Dionne Brand (2001) calls "a tear in the world." Even more than Richard Wright, Dionne Brand in *A Map to the Door of No Return* approaches the question of loss through the problematic of names: "My grandfather said he knew what people we came from. I reeled off all the names I knew. Yoruba? Ibo? Ashanti? Mandingo? He said no to all of them, saying that he would know it if he heard it. I was thirteen. I was anxious for him to remember." Needless to say, her grandfather never remembered, and this inability to find a source of the self becomes "a space" in Brand. But listen to this: "My grandfather could not summon up a vision or landscape or a people which would add up to a name. And it was profoundly disturbing. Having no name to call on was having no past; having no past pointed to a fissure between the past and the present."

Africa. No name. No localizable people. But Dionne Brand and Richard Wright are not alone. The same gaps, the same yawning holes, the same empty spaces characterize imaginaries of the black Diasporic world in Africa. Ask any African to name African America or the Caribbean in any of our languages: Yoruba, Hausa, Igbo, Wolof, Gikuyu. Ask any African when they first came into consciousness of geographies of blackness beyond the African continent in their own native languages and imaginaries. You will get interesting answers.

Interesting answers from, say, this African addressing you right now. My earliest intimations of color and geography were in Yoruba elementary school readers and in the local lores of the Yagba people in Isanlu, my hometown in north-central Nigeria. I grew up suffused in opaque references to something called "ile alawo dudu" (the land of the black-skinned people) which became Africa once we went to school and encountered the same references in the subject called social studies. The conceptual unity of chromatism and geography in the expression, "ile alawo dudu," always stood in a binary opposition to "ile alawo funfun" (the land of the white-skinned people), "ilu oba" (the land of the king/throne) or "ilu oyinbo" (the land of white people).

Please remember that I am still in primary school—or precisely what we call nursery/primary school in Nigeria. Thus far, all references to "oko eru" (slavery), in the quotidian conversation of my elders, referred to the amorphous forms of domestic slavery known to that world. Consequently, between "ile alawo dudu" and "ile alawo funfun," my language conceptualized the world as a site of contestations and confrontations between a very black Africa and a very, very white Euro-America. There simply was no conceptual space yet for our black cousins in the Diaspora.

Right there was a blank space in my language and conceptual world. Growing up, I read a lot of books in my father's library. The story of black people beyond

Africa began to creep gradually into my world. The very idea that there were black people beyond Africa meant that the neat correlation between "ile alawo dudu" and Africa or "ile alawo funfun" and Euro-America in my mother tongue would no longer work. I suddenly had black people beyond Africa to account for and nothing in my language could handle the situation. In Form Two, in Titcombe College, I participated in a state-wide French competition and won a slot to travel to Togo by road with select students from all over Kwara State. I was eleven years old. Somehow, we never made it to Togo but we got as far as Badagry, and our handlers took us on a tour of one of the most important slave ports in West Africa. The Black Atlantic came crashing into my world during that first visit to Badagry at age eleven!

Back home, I asked restless questions from my dad, my mom, my teachers, and even my maternal grandmother, Mama Isanlu. If thousands of black people had been taken across the ocean to faraway lands, as we were told by the tour guides in Badagry, how come the places they were taken to were not part of "ile alawo dudu" (land of the black-skinned people) which meant and still means Africa? If there are so many black people in the Americas, why did our language insist that the place was "ilu oyinbo" or "ile alawo funfun" (the land of whites)? I guess I wanted people to tell me what we called African America or the Caribbean in Yagba and Yoruba now that I knew that black people also inhabited those places.

The answers that I got were slurs that stigmatized a people and did not really describe their land. My grandmother, for instance, spoke in Yagba of "ireke noin" which standard Yoruba would have as "awon ireke" (sugar cane people). The sugar cane plantation had become the shorthand for describing our cousins in the Caribbean. "Akata," the main Yoruba descriptor for African Americans, especially African American women, is equally a slur.

My nagging suspicion is that when the black body politic is seared by the anxiety of contact among black Diasporic people and conceptual poverty among African people, capitalism, the permanent profiteer from black history and misery, smells an opportunity. One such opportunity that capitalism of the basest casino kind has not been able to resist is the unfolding drama of Badagry. Badagry is a small coastal town to the west of Lagos and one of the most important slave ports in West Africa. For reasons that I am yet to ascertain, Badagry is not as famous as other slave ports and doors of no return in Ghana, Senegal, and Angola. Nigeria has never been able to maximize the tourism potential of Badagry and turn it to a Mecca for black people in the Diaspora who troop to doors of no return in Cape Coast and Gorée.

Because Badagry is not as famous as the other slave ports in the sub-region, let me run through a list of what you can expect to see at that site of memory: (1) the Mobee Family Slave Relics Museum, which houses the original relics left by the slave trade, the chains are more six hundred years old, preserved right from when the trade was stopped; (2) the slave market, an open space where slaves were auctioned, also a meeting point for European slavers and African middlemen. At its peak, 46,800 people were sold annually from the market; (3) a slave baracoon, used by Brazilian merchants as a holding cell for slaves; (4) the slave route port, used in the seventeenth and eighteenth centuries, where slaves were moved down to the slave route and finally to the Point of No Return; (5) the Point of No Return, a twenty-five-minute trek on a narrow bush path to the sea.

These are some of the preserved spaces of memory in Badagry. News of the potential desecration of this space of memory first filtered incredulously into the Nigerian public sphere as street gossip. I dismissed the first rumors of desecration outright. Now, who would want to do such a thing? Who would want to place a knife on the solemnity of memory in Badagry?

In his classic essay, "Postmodernism and Consumer Society," Fredric Jameson theorizes everything, every space, as fair game for a "late consumer or multinational capitalism." The new late capitalism described by Jameson has not come empty-handed, to paraphrase Chinua Achebe: It has brought in its wake what Jameson describes as "new types of consumption; planned obsolescence; an ever more rapid rhythm of fashion and styling changes; the penetration of advertising, television and the media generally to a hitherto unparalleled degree throughout society" (1983/1998, p. 19).

Note that what Jameson describes as a "new moment of late consumer or multinational capitalism" would be described as old fashioned by my contemporary undergraduate students because Jameson was writing in 1998—that is at least ten years before Facebook, Twitter, iPod, and iPad.

Should there be a limit to the ubiquity of casino capitalism? Should there be lines too sacred to be crossed? Apparently, some members of the Jackson family don't think so. Unknown to many Americans, Nigeria is to the Jackson family what South Africa is to Oprah Winfrey. The Jacksons have been visiting Nigeria for a very long time. Michael Jackson performed in Nigeria a couple of times; occasionally, his brothers would sneak in and out of Lagos. Eventually, one of them, Marlon Jackson, got a bright idea and approached American developers: turn the Badagry slave port into a luxury resort, complete with a Jackson Five museum, a slavery memorial (thank God!), a luxury hotel, a golf course, and a massage parlor!

What I initially dismissed as rumor was eventually confirmed by the local newspapers. Even the *Guardian* of London got interested and ran this story on February 17, 2009, "Michael Jackson's Brother Plans Slavery Theme Park." Theme park? Echoes of Disneyland? Echoes of Neverland? Let's quote more of the *Guardian*'s report:

> A museum for the Jackson Five is to be built in Nigeria, American developers have announced, as part of a $3.4bn (£2.4bn) luxury resort including concert halls, golf courses, casinos—and a memorial for Africa's former slave trade. The Badagry Historical Resort, located near Badagry's former slave port, will include a multimillion pound memorial, slave history theme park, five-star hotel and Jackson Five museum. The project is supported in part by Marlon Jackson, one of Michael Jackson's brothers. (Michaels, 2009)

American developers? I hope I'm not the only one who gets jittery whenever I hear that "American developers" are moving in somewhere? After all, we know what happens whenever "American developers" move into America's historic neighborHOODS. America is a permanent theater of war between memory and gentrification. Esiaba Irobi, the late Nigerian writer, captures the fate of Harlem in a little-known poem which deserves to be a classic of the Black Atlantic library. In "Harlem," Irobi's poet persona laments that "every living trace of us, our black faces and asses" will disappear under the weight of white capitalist gentrification.

These are just the first three stanzas of a long poem in seven stanzas. I have published an extended essay on the poem that is available online. The sentiment is sufficiently clear. Is this the fate that awaits the sites of memory in Badagry? After all, it is the same American developers deploying the same keywords, the same diction, the same code words from the registers of late consumer capitalism: theme parks, golf courses, massage parlors. We are lucky they aren't talking yet of water slides and roller coasters; we are lucky that they are not yet dreaming of replicating the Las Vegas strip on the historic slave routes of Badagry but don't hold your breath.

The most principled, most memorable line of opposition to this potential act of desecration comes from Toyin Falola, one of Nigeria's most famous ambassadors in American academia. Professor Falola tells the BBC:

It is not appropriate from a cultural or historical point of view. Moneymaking and historical memory are allies in the extension of capitalism. You cry with one eye and wipe it off with a cold beer, leaving the other eye open for gambling. (Walker, 2009)

I couldn't have put it better. But questions persist. The capitalism that we are talking about here is proposing to desecrate memory in Africa because she has been invited by Marlon Jackson, a Diasporic son of Africa. How does this inflect the problematic question of shared memories of slavery between Africans and Diasporic Africans?

In his classic "Between Memory and History: Les Lieux de Mémoire," Pierre Nora (1989) discusses three kinds of memory: archive memory, duty memory, and distance memory. What are the implications of Marlon Jackson's Badagry adventure for duty memory? And then, my final question, a reiteration: should there be lines that capitalism must not cross? I do not know the answer but there are lessons to be learned from Chinua Achebe.

The recent faceoff between Chinua Achebe and the rapper 50 Cent over the latter's attempt to use the title of Africa's most famous novel, *Things Fall Apart* (1958), for a film project goes much deeper than the simple question of the protection of intellectual property. After all, copyright laws do not extend to titles. But 50 Cent comes complete with a certain countercultural symbology that is completely out of whack with the solemn memories inscribed in *Things Fall Apart.* 50 Cent is bling-bling, face cap worn backwards, saggy pants hanging down to expose expensive designer boxer shorts, tattoos, totally ripped six-pack abs, heavily pimped hummers with twenty-eight-inch rims (apologies to Xzibit), and other kinds of toys, cribs, and lyrics projecting a hypersexualized image of the black woman reduced to her posterior. Now, can you imagine *Things Fall Apart* in the candy shop? I'm sure you know that song. I prefer to enjoy it when I go clubbing. Not when I am thinking of a cultural heritage of the importance of *Things Fall Apart.*

50 Cent offered a million dollars. Achebe declined the insult. This tells me that capitalism and profit will never consider any space too sacred to violate. And the stories of 50 Cent and Marlon Jackson warn us to resist the temptation of presenting capitalism and memory as a white versus black affair. If invasive capitalism has any race at all, it is green. Not the green of the environment. The green of the dollar bill. Green is the race of capitalism for now. Tomorrow, the race of capitalism will be the red of the Chinese yuan as America is swept aside by China. A man is entitled to witness the collapse of at least one empire in his lifetime. I was not around when the British Empire collapsed; I will not be around to see the collapse of the

emergent Chinese empire. I am therefore honored to be a living witness of the gradual collapse of the American empire.

But Achebe teaches us that our only hope lies in people who are ready to stand up for memory and say: No! That is what so many Americans are doing in the Occupy movement that has spread across this country like wildfire in the harmattan.

Ode to the Bottle

For Ken Harrow, Who Laughed

My short essay "The ABC of a Nigerian Joke for Western Audiences" (2012) is surprisingly still traveling and acquiring mileage online, especially in spaces of Africanist cultural scholarship in North American academe. Often, I receive an email from a doctoral student or a colleague who has only just stumbled on it and requires some clarification. The said essay was inspired by some white Western Facebook friends who inboxed me, wondering what the fuss was all about as Nigerians and other African nationals cracked up after I had posted a joke that only cultural insiders would understand.

Here's a recap of the joke. A policeman arrests a guy for urinating in a place displaying the commonplace "Do Not Urinate Here" sign in Nigeria. The cop fines the offender five hundred naira. The guy brings out one thousand naira and asks for his change. Says the policeman to the offender: "urinate again. I no get change." I wrote "The ABC of a Nigerian Joke" to explore the postcolonial cultural locatedness of this and other jokes. I made the case that humor is the most difficult thing to translate; it's very untranslatability making it one of the most reliable ways of gauging cultural integration in immigrant and diasporic communities.

Let me explain. I believe that Africans hardly find oyinbo people's jokes funny and vice versa. You, therefore, know that your African friend has truly integrated if he attends one of those gatherings where oyinbo people serve cookies, muffins, slices of pizza, celery, and dip, all displayed beside three jugs of regular coffee, decaf coffee, and hot water for tea respectively, and laughs at the appropriate decibel level when he hears jokes that aren't funny because they are not immediately translatable into his own modes of cultural apprehension.

Appropriate decibel level is very important. If he laughs at the exact decibel level and at exactly the same time as the rest of the room, he is thoroughly acculturated. He has become an African oyinbo man. The jokes of the host culture are genuinely funny to him. After one muffin, one piece of carrot, one piece of celery, and a Styrofoam cup of decaf coffee without sugar, this African may even rub his belly, yawn, and exclaim to his neighbor in the room: "Wow, I'm bursting. There's so much good food here." And he means it. He is genuinely full for even his belly is now Canadian—or American as the case may be—and no longer requires the heavy work out of kenkey, fufu or pounded yam to be full.

However, if his own burst of laughter comes a couple of seconds later than the rest of the room every time something funny is said, if his laughter constantly bursts out a tad louder than the rest of the room, then he is one of those Africans who remind you of the proverb: a tree trunk may spend twenty years in the river, it will never become a crocodile. He is just laughing like an automaton in order not to be the odd one out. The jokes ain't funny. And he is starving as hell. He is merely struggling to blend into that room, cramming muffins, celery, and dip into his mouth and wishing he had taken the precaution of eating poundo and egusi soup at home before leaving for that oyinbo people's party.

"The ABC of a Nigerian Joke" made it to Professor Toyin Falola's famous Pan-Africanist listserv, USAAfricaDialogue. One of the party chieftains of that listserv, Professor Ken Harrow of Michigan State University, one of the most significant Africanist thinkers of our era, a man whose work is my melody in the business of theorizing African literatures and cultures and whose praxis thoroughly inspires, wondered aloud why he laughed on encountering the Nigerian joke about the policeman. Are you for real, I thought, as I read Ken's reaction. Something would be seriously wrong, I thought further, if Ken Harrow, a *vieux routier* of Africa, encountered an African proverb and didn't find it funny. After all, he got to Africa before me and has never really left. I thought he had forgotten his own African insiderhood, earned over decades of meticulous and thorough scholarly labor in the cultural vineyards of the continent. Ken, it should be obvious to you why you laughed, why you found that joke funny, I thought, as I made a mental note of waiting for an inspired moment to pen a follow-up essay—this essay—in his honor.

Midway into a handsome bottle of Beaujolais to celebrate a particularly good news today, December 6, 2012, my brain finally receives the creative bang she has been waiting for in order to undertake this essayistic excursion in popular culture in homage to Ken Harrow. Beyond the earned cultural insiderhood which would open up Nigerian, nay, African humor to an Africanist *vieux routier* like Ken, making him laugh at the joke about a Nigerian policeman and the politics of "change collection" in the postcolonial atmospherics of the checkpoint, there are contact zones and meeting points of the collectively human which, in hindsight, my initial essay, focused on cultural particulars, does not adequately address. As culturally hermetic as humor is, such sites, zones, and spaces of the universally human offer many opportunities for her to cross borders without passport and visa requirements.

The bottle is one such location of the universally shared. I had mentioned the bottle and a London pub in the earlier essay as indices of integration if an African found the jokes there funny. I now hold a different opinion. An African may find jokes in that particular location funny for the reasons I am about to explore. There are universal modes of human sentience organized around the symbology of the bottle and its contents. I am not talking about the bottle in your living room or other private spaces. I am talking about that object in its public lifeworld; in spaces where its phallic posture on the table is generative of sensations, experiences, lore, and cultures that can combine seamlessly into narratives of the universally humorous.

In the American/Canadian corner bar and grill, the Irish/English pub, the French bistro or brasserie, the southern African shebeen (originally Irish), the Ivorian maquis, the Nigerian beer parlor, burukutu, paraga, ogogoro, or shepe spot, the bottle stands as humanity's singular answer to the eternal question of Babel. No deity can create Babel within the cultural actuations or the bottle. In the domain of alcohol, the human experience tells Babel: we are one people, one voice, one language, one humor. Indeed, I have yet to encounter experiences and narratives of the bottle and drunkenness in one culture that cannot be translated to and carried by the idioms of another. In the domain of the bottle, humor is transculturally and transnationally funny.

Indeed, in its very defiance and transcendence of the curse of Babel, the bottle becomes demiurge, creating art—universal art, transnationally funny art—in the figure of the rambler. In country music, the character of the rambler is a player, an irresponsible figure who breaks girls' hearts and never stays. Don Williams (1978) calls him a "rake and ramblin' man" in his song of the same title. Don Williams's rambler knocks up a girl and refuses to accept responsibility because:

You know I'm a rake and ramblin' man . . .

He goes on to complain for good measure that he does not look like a daddy. In Zac Brown Band's (2010) superhit song, "Colder Weather," the rambler is as irresponsible as his elder brother in Don Williams's song. The heartbroken girl who is left behind in Colorado says to the rambler in "Colder Weather":

You're a ramblin' man, you ain't ever gonna change.

If country music condemns the rambler as a patriarchal breaker of female hearts, the bottle redeems him as an archetypal lone figure, a singular human habitus of the universally funny who harms no one. All he does is enact a personal drama of redemption from alcohol—or of redemption through alcohol consumption. Whether he is running away from or toward the bottle, the alcoholic rambler is generative of narratives and experiences which carry humor across cultural and transnational boundaries. In America, we encounter the rambler as the redemption-seeking persona in Tom Paxton's (1967) classic folk song, "Bottle of Wine":

Bottle of wine, fruit of the vine, when you gonna let me get sober?

Paxton's rambler self-identifies as an abject American alcoholic constantly in search of nickels and dimes. Now, why does generation after generation of French citizens go about in France believing that this funny, all-American rambler is French? It speaks to the translatability of the idioms and humor of the bottle. Graeme Allwright, a New Zealand singer who moved to France in 1948 and subsequently became a famous French singer, translated Tom Paxton's song to French and released it in France as "jolie bouteille." It became and still is one of the greatest hits of the French folk tradition. What got lost in translation—wiped clean from French memory—is the fact that "jolie bouteille" is a mere adaptation/translation of an American original by Tom Paxton. In essence, the American rambler has been so seamlessly appropriated by the French, who converted him to a flâneur and sent him on errands of redemption from the bottle, with zero trace of his American origin. If only Tom Paxton had thought of making the rambler drink Budweiser instead of a bottle of wine!

Why is the transition from rambler to flâneur so easy? The answer is simple. One may be a consumer of cheap and inferior California wine in America while the other consumes superior merlot in France, their narratives and experiences of the bottle generate humor that can find a natural home in any culture. Hence, we encounter this alcoholic rambler in the Yoruba imagination. Also a loner like his American and French booze-cousins, he is however not seeking redemption from the bottle. He is defiant. His redemption lies in claiming the bottle like the portion of the Nigerian Pentecostal Christian. He is wealthier than his Western cousins in America and France and does not need to sing for nickels and dimes to be able to afford his booze. Thus, the Yoruba rambler gets to boast in Kollington Ayinla's song:

A f'owo mu oti ki ku s'ode, gere, ng o dele mi o.

According to Kollington's rambler, no matter how badly a drunk who spends his own money on booze staggers, he will somehow make his way home. Ebenezer Obey's rambler ups the ante. Like Kollington's, he is also wealthier than the American rambler and the French flâneur. He is not seeking redemption *from* but *through* the bottle. He is not sure that alcohol consumption is legal in heaven; hence, he evinces the imperative of the earthly precaution:

Haba ma muti l'aiye nbi . . . Boya won ki mu l'orun.

Obey's rambler does not doubt the ability of hedonism here on earth to take him to heaven. His only problem is the fear of the unknown: will there be alcohol in heaven when I die and go there? However, he is not going to travel to that celestial destination via the way, the truth, and the life proposed by the Christian Bible. In his humoristic transgressions, Obey's rambler is clearly a man who could easily earn an OBE from the Queen of England in recognition of the earthly Eucharistic gloss he has placed on drunkenness, that very English of national traits. Speaking of English drunkenness, Elizabeth Renzetti writes in Canada's *Globe and Mail* newspaper:

The English have more words for drunk than the Inuit have for snow, perhaps because it is as much part of the landscape. On a given night, you might be bladdered, legless, paralytic or rotten with drink. . . . I thought I'd heard them all until British Home Secretary Theresa May used the phrase "preloaded" on Friday to announce her government's war on binge drinking. Preloading refers to the act of getting hammered before you go out to get hammered—that is stocking up on cheap booze from the grocery store in order to be good and wobbly by the time you hit the bars.

Now, why am I in stitches reading Renzetti's description of the English? The Canadian is making this Nigerian laugh by describing the English in registers that are brokered by the universal signifyin' of the bottle. If she makes me laugh, I am sure she is immensely capable of making Ken Harrow, the American, laugh with precisely the same registers. American, Canadian, French, English, Nigerian: the bottle speaks only one language but we can all understand it in our respective languages. The bottle is not Babel. She is Pentecost. We all hear her speak in our respective languages.

Aso Ebi on My Mind

I t was one of those auspicious summer days when the horribly English weather of Vancouver, British Columbia, uncharacteristically decides to wear a tropical smile. Sometimes there is a computer glitch in heaven, and the sun mysteriously defies all that dour, cloy, and gray wetness and marches across the permanent penumbra that the residents of Vancouver call the sky. For those unable to afford that vital occasional escape to the tropical heat and brightness of Mexico or Hawai'i, such rare sun-sodden days offer an occasion to spill into the streets, city parks, or fan across Vancouver's famous beaches.

For the African in Vancouver, the sun whispers one word, only one word to the soul: home. "The Negro Speaks of Rivers" says Langston Hughes (1921), that famous African American poet of the Harlem Renaissance. That, perhaps, is true for the uprooted black of the New World for whom rivers and the Atlantic Ocean—any moving mass of water—hold a special historical resonance. For the contemporary Diasporic African whose immediate identity is rooted, not in rosy memories of the giant strides of ancient empires and kingdoms, just before Kunta Kinte boarded the

Keynote lecture delivered at the African Textiles Exhibition of Carleton University's Arts Gallery, February 16, 2011 ship to Annapolis, Maryland, but in the immediate actualities of the nation-states that emerged from the trauma of colonialism between 1957 and 1994, remembrance of the vivifying essence of the African sun—the famous African warmth when it becomes metaphor—always comes before rivers. In the unforgiving coldness of Euro-America, we huddle together to remember and speak of the warmth and heat of Africa, not necessarily of the luminous currents of the Nile, the Niger, the Congo, and the Zambezi.

Because the continent's heat and warmth have allowed us to evolve a culture of the public space and the street as year-long sites for the expression and instantiation of culture—dance, music, celebrations, rituals, festivals, and myriad forms of aesthetic revelry—the occasionally bright and sunny day in a city such as Vancouver is always an opportunity for what I call instant-mix jollification by the African community. For those of us in the Diaspora, a sunny day is always an excuse to try and reproduce poor photocopies of continental public festivities that our people back home take for granted. You call up a few friends and the African thing takes its full colorful course. To any observer from a distance, these activities may look like any regular Western barbecue gathering or community center event. You won't have to listen for a long time before you discover that the difference lies in the decibel level for Africa, especially Nigeria, insists on not partying quietly. If you've got the culture, flaunt it. No apologies.

And so it was that on this particular sunny day in Vancouver during my years as a doctoral student in that city, a Nigerian friend and I were returning home from a party when we noticed a group of gaily dressed men and women having a nice time in one of the city's public parks. More than the great weather and the sight of what to us could be any group of Africans partying in an open public park, something else attracted us to that motley crowd and I will come to that presently. First, let us examine the instinctive reaction of my friend. I was driving, he beside me in the passenger seat. We see the party group from a distance and my friend exclaims: "Ol'boy, e be like say e dey happen over there o. Na Naija people sef. Abeg make we go chop awoof." Never mind that we had just left a party!

Needless to say, I agreed with his assessment, and we soon started looking for a parking space. By now, every Nigerian in this room already understands where my friend and I are coming from and where I am going with this analysis. "Ol'boy, e be like say e dey happen over there o." Nothing extraordinary here. That is just an observation that a party was probably going on. The clincher—and I need you to pay attention here—lies in the next two sentences. "Na Naija people sef." That's my friend already declaring with absolute certainty that the party people we had just seen were Nigerians. Remember, we are still in the car, looking for parking. We hadn't seen any familiar faces. How could he possibly have known? At this stage, that group could still reasonably be from any part of sub-Saharan Africa. Then comes his last sentence: "abeg make we go chop awoof." That's Nigerian-speak for the Canadian: "let's help ourselves to some free food."

Nigerians and Africans in this room will probably complain that I have ruined that fantastic African cultural peculiarity just by translating it to Canadian English. Let's help ourselves to some free food—that sounds so ordinary and hollow. Render that statement in any African language and in the proper contexts and an entire universe of meaning comes alive, totally untranslatable to Western audiences, bearing stories of Africa's legendary philosophy of hosting and hospitality. The Yoruba, an ethnic nationality of some forty million people in southwestern Nigeria—not counting their kith and kin in West Africa and the New World from Bahia to Cuba via Barbados and Trinidad—have gone a step ahead by reducing that continental philosophy to one catchy expression: "mo gbo mo ya." Again, I must commit the heresy of translating the untranslatable: "I heard about your party so I'm crashing in on it."

In essence, when you see twenty Africans gathered in a party or a reception, chances are that only six of them were formally invited. The rest are probably exercising the cultural license of "mo gbo mo ya." It is a very bad African indeed who invites six people to a party and goes ahead to prepare food and drinks for the six just because they all RSVPed. Your ability to envisage and provide for the uninvited sixteen—most of whom you probably have never met before because the friend of a friend of your in-law's nephew invited them to your party without telling you—is a crucial cultural proposition.

This explains why my friend and I parked the car and approached an open air party to which we were not invited, walking magisterially like we were the mayor of Vancouver. We joined the group and got the sort of loud, effusive, and absolutely warm African reception we expected. But it was immediately obvious to us that we had made a mistake in our initial assessment of their national identity. My friend had uttered "Naija people" when we spotted the party group, and I had concurred. How do you explain our error? How to explain that two Nigerians mistook a group of Africans partying on a bright summer day in a Vancouver park for Nigerians?

I can picture the answer in the minds of some of our African brothers and sisters in this room: well, it is like you Nigerians to think that Africa starts in Calabar and ends in Maiduguri. Well, we did not make that mistake out of the habit of believing that Nigeria is Africa and Africa is Nigeria. Our error came from the vestimentary splendor of the women in the group: those Sierra Leonean women were all dressed in what any Nigerian would immediately recognize as aso ebi!

Aso Ebi, that famous Nigerian cultural testament, was the culprit that induced the error of mistaking Sierra Leoneans for Nigerians from a distance. Many Nigerians in Euro-America have similar tales of encountering aso ebi among nationals of other African countries. Nigeria's cultural transnationalism and globalism are not just about Nollywood. Aso ebi is inflecting vestimentary styles and aesthetics all over Africa and the Diaspora. Because aso ebi immediately evokes imagery of party crowds and carnivalesque street revelry, it is perhaps apposite that we say a thing or two about crowds before we probe the cultural warrens of aso ebi any further.

This is a particularly auspicious time to talk about crowds because North African crowds, seeking freedom and political agency, have invaded our living rooms and other private spaces lately. Television and the internet have taken us to the streets of Tunis, Cairo, and now Algiers. I tell you, listening to Western pundits and commentators go on and on about these auspicious developments in North Africa is pure torture. From London to Washington via Ottawa, we are being told by condescending commentators, ignorant as usual of the trajectory of the crowd in their own immediate history and culture, that the African crowd is finally learning the ropes and picking the praxis of political and cultural expression from paths already beaten by the Western crowd.

Crowds—or the masses, as modernist discourse referred to them—have not always been the organic entity whose right to the pursuit of happiness, we are told, the democratic Western state exists to guarantee with all sorts of welfare packages. As they built modernism and its associated cultures in all spheres of existence in the nineteenth century, European intellectuals, going all the way back to the legacy of Nietzsche, despised crowds and the masses as polluters of culture. The cultural critic, John Carey, has given us the most fascinating account of the epistemological violence that the intellectual inventors of Western modernism visited on crowds and the masses. The advent of crowds, masses, and mass culture was viewed as a clear and present danger to high culture by a European intelligentsia that proceeded to constantly try and raise the level of culture and the arts beyond the reach of the ordinary people.

Nietzsche had many heirs in the nineteenth and twentieth centuries. In no particular order, everyone from José Ortega y Gasset to T. S. Eliot via Hermann

Hesse, Gustave Flaubert, André Gide, H. G. Wells, George Bernard Shaw, Evelyn Waugh, D. H. Lawrence, W. B. Yeats, weighed in on the menace of crowds, mass culture, and even mass literacy. Everything that could make cultivation of the mind easily available to and accessible by the masses—newspapers, radio—was contemptuously dismissed by the modernist crowd whose aim was to write the people out of the history of the production of culture. Hear John Carey (1993):

> The intellectuals could not, of course, actually prevent the masses from attaining literacy. But they could prevent them reading literature by making it too difficult for them to understand—and this is what they did. The early twentieth century saw a determined effort, on the part of the European intelligentsia, to exclude the masses from culture. In England this movement has become known as modernism. In other European countries it was given different names, but the ingredients were essentially similar, and they revolutionized the visual arts as well as literature. Realism of the sort that it was assumed the masses appreciated was abandoned. So was logical coherence. Irrationality and obscurity were cultivated.

But even this is still good news. As modernism pursued its inexorable course in European culture, the prism through which she viewed European masses began to border dangerously on lunacy. Thus it was that Ortega y Gasset would opine that modern art must divide the public into two distinct and antagonistic classes: those who can understand and those who cannot. Naturally, those who can understand art belong in the category of the chosen few; those who cannot belong in the category of the inferior masses. John Carey sees a natural progression from the arrogance of modernism to the sophistry of the avant-garde among the European intelligentsia:

> As an element in the reaction against mass values the intellectuals brought into being the theory of the avant-garde, according to which the mass is, in art and literature, always wrong. What is truly meritorious in art is seen as the prerogative of a minority, the intellectuals, and the significance of this minority is reckoned to be directly proportionate to its ability to outrage and puzzle the mass. Though it usually purports to be progressive, the avant-garde is consequently always reactionary. That is, it seeks to take literacy and culture away from the masses.

I could go on and on about modernism's and the avant-garde's representation of and attitude to European masses but those of you who have read the great texts of that age are sufficiently familiar with that scenario. Suffice it to say that the science of that age was not deaf to the language of the poets and the philosophers of Europe. Hence we began to hear of projects such as Tom Harrison's Mass Observation which reduced lower people to scientific specimen; we began to hear of the masses being compared with bacteria. It just so happens that there was a fellow named Adolf Hitler who was listening to all of that philosophico-scientific discourse on lower peoples and crowds with keen interest. Across the Atlantic, the European diaspora in America was also listening to what their elder brothers were saying back home in Europe about lower people and classes and began to develop a healthy appetite for the "science" of eugenics . . .

If Europeans of a certain class could treat their own masses and crowds this way, what would they not do to the "natives" that they were busy manufacturing at the time in India and all over Africa? They carried the same modernist and avant-gardist arrogance to the theaters of empire and colonial violence and tried to impose a certain genteel Victorianism on everybody and everything in sight. This is where they failed. Modernist and avant-gardist arrogance met their cultural nemesis in Africa for Africa had a different way of looking at crowds and the masses.

Those of you who have read Chinua Achebe will understand what I am talking about. Think of *Things Fall Apart* (1958) and *Arrow of God* (1964). Think of all those communal celebrations and ritualistic feasts in the novels. How do you separate the people from all of that? How do you elevate the new yam festival above the people? How do you begin to rewrite the peoples of Africa as impediments to all the cultural enactments that the continent is famous for? How do you go to Yoruba land in southwest Nigeria and tell the people that culture and its street expression must be elevated above their heads? We are talking of a people whose philosophy of the ownership of culture is expressed in the processional hymn that the Yoruba here in this audience will sing along with me:

Awa yio s'oro ile wa o . . . esin kan o pe, k'awa ma s'oro. (Jones, Thorpe, & Wootton, 2008, p. 190)

This homiletic call to ritual observance firmly locates the ownership of culture in the *idile* (family unit in a much extended sense). How do you take this away from the *idile* in an avant-gardist move to relocate culture on higher grounds? This explains why the Yoruba would teach Euromodernism a lesson or two in the ownership of culture and the treatment of crowds. The Yoruba would not evolve an ethos of culture in which the people would progressively be treated as bacteria, a blight on high culture. Rather, even in the context of colonial rape and the succeeding context of postcolonial atrophy supervised by local buffoons who have ruled Nigeria since independence, the Yoruba have always insisted that the crowd is the owner of culture, especially in its more expressive, aesthetic, and performative dimensions of "miliki," "faaji," and "ariya."

I am again confronted by the burden of translation, and I'm afraid that I must do further violence to African untranslatables by rendering those three as "jollification." Or joie de vivre for those of you in the upper classes! When these three instances of jollification—"miliki," "faaji," and "ariya"—combine in the streets of Lagos, Ibadan, Akure, Ondo, Ijebu Ode, Abeokuta, or Osogbo, the result is the Yoruba party phenomenon now famously known all over the world as "owambe." I am of course exploring a people's different take on crowds and the location of culture. I am claiming that whereas nineteenth and twentieth-century Europe treated crowds and the people contemptuously as her modernist and avant-gardist cultures developed, and exported those condescending attitudes to the empire, Africa responded by insisting on a different location and ownership of culture.

In essence, while the crowds were being treated contemptuously and written out of culture by European intelligentsia, the Yoruba would deck that crowd in aso ebi and send them to the streets of Yorubaland as the owners and carriers of culture, color, and aesthetics. In owambe and aso ebi, the people, and not the intelligentsia, are the arbiters of taste. To surrender agency to the people in the areas of pleasure and jouissance as the Yoruba do with owambe and aso ebi is to be in fundamental consonance with the idea of democracy as the will of the people.

I bring in the idea of the will of the people and collective identification with an ideal or a goal in order to move beyond regular conceptualizations which limit aso ebi to the rapturous collective uniforms of crowds or specific groups within crowds during festive occasions: weddings, funerals, house warmings, naming ceremonies, thanksgiving, and the manifold occasions of "washing": Nigerians "wash" everything from the purchase of a new car to promotion at work, from the purchase of a bigger electric generator to the arrival of that all-important life-saving visa to Britain, America—or Canada where the first two preferences fail. Depending on economic circumstances, any of these instances is an occasion for aso ebi.

The presence of Nigerian women in this audience obviously means that I can conveniently continue to theorize and forget to define aso ebi, who buys it, and why it is bought, who sews it and where it is sewn, its composition from the gele to the iro via, the buba, and the pele. Trust me, all of those details will emerge during question and answer. Suffice it to say here that will and agency enter into the picture because you must first subscribe to the validity of whatever is being celebrated before agreeing to be part of the aso ebi–wearing crowd. At a fundamental level, aso ebi is always a form of identification with communal ethos, with the collective. Aesthetics and color enter into the picture when one beholds the resplendence of it all.

With seventy-six thousand entries the last time I checked, Google is obviously not doing too badly on the aso ebi terrain. However, if you are a careful reader, you will notice a refrain common to virtually all the Google entries. Here is, in fact, how one Google entry which calls itself *Urban Dictionary* defines it:

> **aso ebi** (*pronounced* ASHO EYBEE)
>
> Nigerian outfits made from matching fabric to be worn by a group of people to a party, wedding, or funeral as a uniform. Wearing a certain aso ebi identifies the group of wearers. For instance, at a wedding, all the bride's friends might wear blue and gold, the bride's family might wear white and gold, and the groom's friends might wear black and pink, and so on. Usually at weddings, the various fabrics for the aso ebi are decided by the bride, and are then announced to all the guests months in advance so they can prepare their outfits. Guests are usually expected to buy the aso ebi from the bride, but close friends and family members and certain prominent individuals may be presented with the aso ebi as a gift. Aso ebi for parties and funerals are generally simple, but aso ebi for weddings may involve many complex changes with entirely different aso ebi for different days of the wedding, and for the reception. (Lotana, 2008)

Urban Dictionary even goes on to avail us of three examples of the aso ebi usage in sentences:

- My five best friends and I all wore aso ebi to my sister's wedding.
- I know I was invited to the wedding but I can't afford the aso ebi so I'm not going.
- What stunning aso ebi!

So far so good. I agree with *Urban Dictionary,* but I must draw your attention to the fact that this definition, like virtually every other description I found online, defines aso ebi as a Nigerian and not a Yoruba phenomenon. For good reason. But the unmistakable and undeniable Yoruba words "aso ebi" denote family cloth or uniform (I hate translating these things).

The phenomenon crossed the cultural boundaries of the Yoruba world a long time ago and, like Nollywood and Pidgin English, was mainstreamed as one of the key elements of Nigeria's national culture. I stand to be corrected, but I do not know of Nigerian ethnic nationalities that are strangers to aso ebi. Nigerian men of non-Yoruba ethnic extraction, especially those who mouth off in internet forums, may complain and grumble loudly about it as a negative influence and dismiss the unending parties of the Yoruba, they will still have to return home in the evening to wives waiting impatiently to nag them for money about a long overdue aso ebi payment. For aso ebi may not have caught the attention of the Benetton Group in order to become part of the United Colors of Benetton, it certainly is a prime candidate for a united colors of Nigeria.

But aso ebi and its associated cultural practices did not stop within the borders of Nigeria. It spread and like Harold Macmillan's wind of change, it has blown over much of the continent in the past five decades, taking on local inflections and adaptations from Ghana to Liberia, Gambia to Zambia. Needless to say, it has spread to the Diaspora, hence the mistake my friend and I made when we saw Sierra Leonean women in aso ebi in Vancouver in the summer of 1999. If culture is Africa's most formidable export at the table of globalization, Nigeria is certainly present at that table with Nollywood and aso ebi, just beside Ghana's kente and Congo's la SAPE. My own pet theory on the phenomenal success of aso ebi here in the African Diaspora is that there is just something about the arresting visual power of the gele—the female headgear component of aso ebi.

It is not for nothing that the gele is by far the most celebrated of aso ebi components in songs, odes, and panegyrics. What Yoruba or Nigerian woman can forget this ever-green chorus, which must now endure the torture of my poor singing talent:

E wo gele gen ge lori aji gbo t'oko.[2]

The song celebrates the famous Yoruba female head gear (the gele), while figuring it in an economy of gender relations as the true marker of a devoted wife. Perhaps it

---

2. See Tampan-Olaitan Theatre Group (2013, March 6), Facebook [Post]. Retrieved from https://www.facebook.com/567934169890898/posts/e-wo-gele-genge-lori-a-ji-gbo-tokoe-wo-gele-genge-lori-a-ji-gbo-tokoaye-ni-o-n-j/568576806493301/

is in recognition that in aso ebi the celebration of cultural genius meshes with style and agency, so that King Sunny Ade, one of Nigeria's great cultural ambassadors on the music front, served notice that the peoples' expression of culture is here to stay. For he warned us that:

> Ariya has no end . . . ariya is unlimited.

In essence, so long as there is aso ebi, there will never be an end to festivals, socialization, and cultural jouissance.

Ara Eko, Ara Oke

Lagos, Culture, and the Rest of Us

Every generation loves to articulate a border identity in Nigeria. Never mind Wole Soyinka's dissing of his own generation as a wasted one. In the nature of things, your generation always just happens to be the last best generation before whatever value systems or institutions you are discussing collapsed irredeemably, hence the tendency to dismiss the generation after you contemptuously. For instance, I belong to a generation of Nigerians that is always grumbling about the perverse values of those Facebook and Twitter addicts now in their twenties and their teens. When two or three Nigerians in their thirties or forties are gathered, they abuse Nigeria's rulers, discuss football, before grumbling about the generation of Nigerians in their twenties and below.

You hear members of my generation gloating about how we were the last ones to be raised by parents with strong moral and ethical values in Nigeria. You hear talk that we were the last who got beaten by our parents if we came home from school with a ten-kobo coin in our pocket whose origin we could not account for (today, a twenty-year-old can just drive from Lagos to the village in a brand-new Hummer, no

Keynote Lecture delivered at a symposium convened by the Nigerian High Commission, Ottawa, Canada, on the theme "Rural-Urban Migration: Nigeria in a Global Context," March 2010.

questions asked); we were the last who had to read books. We grumble that these young ones in their twenties now are so allergic to reading that you could hardly get them to read one book per year. Contributing to such beer and chicken wings pub discussions, I would claim that the best gifts I got as a teenager were titles from the African Writers Series. Now, to gain the attention of my younger ones in Nigeria, the gift has to be a BlackBerry or an iPod, definitely not a book.

We forget that the generation just before us—those mostly now in their fifties —is perhaps saying exactly the same uncomplimentary things about us, believing, just like us, that they are the last best generation to happen to Nigeria. Suffice it to say that I feel sufficiently enamored to exploit the outlined generational border dynamics, albeit jokingly, and declare that mine was the last generation that attended Titcombe College, Egbe, when Titcombe was Titcombe! After us, the deluge and the locust years! The regular story of Nigeria's institutional collapse became the portion of Titcombe College—apologies to Pentecostals! Titcombe wasn't just Titcombe when we enrolled in the early eighties because of the exceptionally high quality of secondary education she offered, she was Titcombe because of the multicultural mosaic of peoplehood that she assembled. The average classroom of thirty-five to forty students boasted enrollment from all the then nineteen states of the federation. Every classroom in the Titcombe of my time was a miniature Nigeria on display.

The senior prefect when I was in Form One was a Benjamin Okoro. My own Form 1C boasted last names like Idongesit, Akpan, Nwaobia, Dowyaro, Zom, Argungu, Okereke, Ajamufua, Whyte, Jackson, and Etomi. The teaching staff comprised an even broader mix of nationalities. Our teachers came from all over the world. Apart from Nigerian teachers, there were the whites: Mr. and Mrs. Balinsky from Canada, Mr. Finch from America, Mrs. Bamigboye from Holland. There were lots of Indian teachers, but I remember now only Mr. and Mrs. Anthony and Mr. Thomas; there were Chinese and Filipino teachers whose names I no longer remember. Then there were the Ghanaians, the dreaded Mr. Inkumsah and the gentler Mr. Badu who taught fine arts. Needless to say, all these foreign teachers had their kids enrolled with us in our classrooms. With such a cosmopolitan mix of staff and studentry, the terroristic "Do Not Speak Vernacular" injunction was virtually useless. You had to speak English anyway.

The Lagosians came with a psychology that requires closer attention. I still do not know—and I need to research this—why Titcombe College attracted that many number of students of Lagos state origin. I am not just talking about students who came from Lagos because their parents were domiciled there but autochthonous Lagosians. They always came to Titcombe in droves. And with them our rude introduction to one of Nigeria's most atavistic forms of the rural-urban binary. For the Lagos contingent believed, paradoxically, that their provincialism was proof of their superiority to "awon ara oke"—rural dwellers or bush people. Most of us had been to Lagos. But you went to Lagos to spend "long vac" with your immediate or extended family members domiciled there. You had little or no contact with the provincialist psychology of the autochthonous Lagosian who was now your classmate in Titcombe College.

The provincialism of this Lagosian is better explored in contrast with the sociology of those of us who formed the non-Lagos population of Titcombe. The average student had family scattered all over northern Nigeria, the middle belt, the southeast, and the south-south and would most likely have been to cities like Sokoto, Kaduna, Kano, Maiduguri, Yola, Minna, Makurdi, Benin, Warri, Enugu, Port Harcourt, and Calabar. There was always an uncle or an aunty or some other distant relative in one of these cities that you were told was inviting you for your next long vac. In addition to this scenario, I accompanied my Dad, one of those Spartan missionary-colonial secondary school principals, on his peripatetic trips across the country to attend his ANCOPSS conventions. He took me along on his trips because he always preached the educational value of travel.

This means that most of us non-Lagosians came to Titcombe already vastly socialized into the divergent cultural richness of the various peoples of Nigeria. We had eaten their food and had been humanized by their ways of seeing and being. Every trip to a different cultural horizon was a new world gained. Years later, my university discipline would teach me that what I was doing then was exploring and being enriched by the world of the Other. I was acquiring cultural capital. I personally had never met anybody completely marooned within their own cultural and spatial geography until I met and made friends with the first real "Lagos people" in Form One. Coming to Titcombe College was almost always their first ever travel outside of the city limits of Lagos!

But they came with an attitude. You could see it written all over their faces that they were wondering which deity they offended to make their parents bundle them out of their beloved Lagos to attend secondary school in a village in the middle of nowhere in the then Kwara State—Titcombe is now in Kogi State. Looking back now, I think the contempt between the Lagos crowd and the rest of us was mutual. Theirs was a conceptualization of the world that reduced the immensity and diversity of Nigeria to one grand narrative of chaotic, garbage-ridden, and rickety modernity called Lagos—Fashola was still a long way off! Everything and everyone outside of their world was bush—the "ara oke" that a cruel fate and the Christian egalitarianism of the Canadians of the Sudan Interior Mission (SIM), led by the Reverend Thomas Titcombe, had dumped onto their sophisticated paths.

For us, we were meeting folks who knew nothing about the rest of that vast country and were therefore monocultural. We found their reductionist purview and the limited scope of their experiential references tiring. Our school kids' anecdotes and experiences extended from Abakaliki to Zungeru via Ibadan, theirs extended from Lagos to Lagos via Lagos. Just as Americans give you a feeling that it is your responsibility to know America and not theirs to know the rest of the world, the ignorance of our classmates from Lagos came with a haughty arrogance: it was our responsibility to know Lagos and not their responsibility to know Nigeria. During break time brawls, some of them would declare with authority that nothing out of Lagos was worth knowing: "mi ni mi de ti so fun won pe ko si ibi to dabi Eko."

Because many of our Lagos classmates came from the upper-middle class to the apex of the class structure in Ikoyi and Victoria Island, their conception of modernity, polish, refinement, and culture devolved from the genteel Victorianism of their parents—identity traits that we now categorize as "aje butter." They brought to Titcombe a rarefied version of Lagos that excluded everything from Ajegunle to Oshodi, Abule Egba to Okokomaiko. They brought a version of culture that was threatened by the bush. They had Humpty Dumpty and Mary's little lamb; we had ijapa (tortoise) and all his adventures in our folktales.

To this day, much of what the Nigerian understands and accepts as cultural refinement and polish still devolves from the values, tastes, and perceptions of this genteel Victorian class that spreads from the Lagos high society to top government circles in Abuja via the narrow circles of Nigerian corporatism. Crumbs of what this upper class considers as modernity move to classes below them by sedimentation. Today, when you encounter the Lagosian who still traffics ignorantly in the passé "ara Eko" versus "ara oke" opposition, especially in the rarefied circles of online conversations among educated and enlightened Nigerians, he is most likely coming from a conceptualization of culture, polish, and cosmopolitanism informed by the apish Victorianism of the Lagos genteel class that those Lagosian classmates of mine and their parents foisted on Titcombe College years ago.

This, of course, represents crass ignorance. As usual, the Westerners who introduced upper-class Nigerians to the sort of genteel Victorianism on display when Dimeji Bankole leads House discussions in his nasalized Britico accent have long left this category of copy-copy Nigerians behind. For this class of Nigerians, culture, refinement, and polish are exclusively about returning home to Ikoyi, Victoria Island, or Lekki from a golf game to evening dinner receptions where they listen to Beethoven, drink cabernet sauvignon, perrier, latté, and espresso; discuss Laz Ekwueme's last conducting of Mozart's Symphony No.4 in D Major; discuss their acquisition of some unknown European painter's work (proudly displayed on the wall) during their last summer vacation in London; the women throw in the latest gossip from the haute-couture worlds of Milan, Paris, and New York, while scheming to make it into the next issue of Dele Momodu's Ovation or to be profiled at www.bellanaija.com.

Because I have access to some of these circles of old money and genteel culture in Lagos, the student of culture in me is always busy and extremely attentive at their gatherings, comparing their "aje butter" mores and mannerisms with those of their oyinbo teachers in London and Paris. Let us settle for Paris for the obvious reason that the French are sufficiently arrogant to consider themselves at the apex of Western culture and civilization. They look down on all other Europeans, especially the English across the channel; they have zilch regard for America and Canada because they do not believe that North American Caucasians are cultured. Not even Glen Gould's global fame makes them think that Canada is cultured.

So, what do the French notions of *homme de culture* (man of culture) and *société de culture* (milieu of culture) mean, and how have they evolved notably in the twentieth and twenty-first centuries? Before 1968, the *homme de culture* who circulated at the highest levels of culture and civilization was like his peers in the West despite his French superiority complex: polished, refined, genteel, manners, taste, elegance, books, opera, vintage wine, baguette, cheese, caviar, pâté, specialist coffee, museums, art collections. Add savoir faire to savoir vivre and you get the picture of what dinner gatherings and soirées looked like in Paris among this class of French *cultivés*.

By the 1950s, new cultural energies were being released all over the Western world that would radically inflect what it means to be cultured and cosmopolitan forever. This means that by the time the emergent elite in Lagos was being born into uppity and snobbish Victorianism in the build-up to independence, by the time they were learning their funny affectation of British and, later, American accents, the owners of the culture were already moving on. The Nigerian elite was manufactured by the British into conceptions of cultural polish that emerged from the Enlightenment, were consolidated by modernity, and had run out of steam by the time the Mr. Follow-Follow Nigerians in the upper class arrived on the scene speaking chaotic Britico and Americana accents through their sophisticated noses. Today, their children are still talking like that in Lagos.

The 1950s unleashed the era of cultural libertinism that would explode in the 1960s and undermine rarefied conceptions of culture. The cultural vocabulary of that era came to be defined by the ways of being and seeing of hitherto excluded and countercultural groups like the beat generation (beatniks), rock 'n'roll, and youth subculture. In the ensuing struggle for the meaning of culture, manners, taste, elegance, books, opera, vintage wine, baguette, cheese, caviar, pâté, specialist coffee, museums, and art collections discovered that they now had to contend with sex, the pill, marijuana, LSD, guns, Afros, T-shirts, and jeans. Welcome to Hippiedom where kitsch and grundge became the new cool and Savile Row suits had to adapt. Sushi and General Tso's chicken would invade the space of culture later to further complicate matters. The shift in cultural vocabulary during this era is neatly captured in "Howl," that great and famous poem by Allen Ginsberg that seemed to have won the struggle for the soul of culture for the little people on the streets of America.

The explosion of cultural libertinism in America was also affecting Europe and things finally exploded in France and other parts of that continent in 1968 when French youths, philosophers, and public intellectuals took to the streets to reject stifling models of society. Culture in Europe and America would never look back after 1968. Events on the political scene ensured this. After having their asses thoroughly whipped by the Vietnamese at the Battle of Dien Bien Phu, the French discovered that noodles, dumplings, and sticky rice were not unworthy items in discussions of haute cuisine; they would make pretty much the same humbling discovery about méchoui, merguez, couscous, tajine, and other elements in Arabo-Magbrebian cuisine after also having their asses whipped in Algeria.

In essence, as imperialism and colonialism disappeared, what began to emerge globally were not just new nation-states all over the Third World but also the hitherto repressed and despised cultures of indigenous peoples. Elements from the cultures of "ara oke" were making it into cultural conversations in the West and forcefully demanding recognition. Knowledge of and competence in them began to determine who was cultured. In academia, this marked the postmodern and the postcolonial turn and the valuation of multiculturalism. With the emergence of the cultures of Africa, Asia, Latin America, and their stubborn claim to a place in the sun, the nature of the French soirée began to change.

Dinner was no longer just about inviting the culturati to the delectation of exclusive French haute cuisine under huge chandeliers in a room with original Louis XIV dining chairs and dining table, a Picasso and a Matisse hanging on the wall, Georges Brassens singing softly in the background. Today, there may also be Ivorian attiéké, aloko (dodo in Nigeria), and Senegalese maafe on that dinner table, just between the bouillabaisse and the gigot. On the wall, between Picasso and Matisse, may be paintings of artists from Tahiti to Zanzibar. Georges Brassens and Beethoven would have lost their monopoly in the CD player to a rotation with kora and balafon music from Sahelian Africa, Andean flute music from Latin America, and oud instrumentals from the Middle East.

Cultured conversation is at the heart of the French high dinner experience. It has to be because dinner could easily last five hours from apéritif to dessert. Do not be surprised that the French culturati gathered around that dinner table may have heard of the paintings of Marcia Kure, Olu Oguibe, Victor Ekpuk, and Victor Ehikhamenor whereas their counterparts around similar dinner tables in Lekki, Ikoyi, and Victoria Island can only offer drab conversation about the London art scene; do not be surprised that some of them have dropped "primitive" in their discussions of the impact of indigenous art on Gauguin (Tahiti) and Picasso (Africa); do not be surprised that these French men and women will listen with very rapt attention if you introduce burukutu and paraga as topics of cultured discourse. They will ask you pertinent questions about the sociology of both drinks, make you describe their color, texture, taste, aroma, what roots and leaves are mixed in paraga and why. Obviously, I am speaking from experience here.

While everyone is pretending to know more about champagne and French wine than the owners of the culture, try introducing paraga and burukutu talk to a high dinner conversation in Lagos if you are even privileged enough to be invited to such tight circles in the first place. Yawa go gas for you. Depending on how high-end the circle is, try speaking a Nigerian language at any point or even try English without a trace of Britico and Americana accent and you could be in trouble. The dinner table in Paris is looking for how to be competent in discussing the cultures of "ara oke" as proof of cosmopolitanism and cultural eclecticism, the civilized "ara Eko" is locked in the past, thumbing his nose at such cultures, and feeling insulted if he hears such lowly Africans speak their "dialect" while cleaning airport toilets in the West. And you go online and encounter him, who sits down in Toronto to wax eloquent about what is cultured and what is crude, his conceptualization of culture wholly informed by the otiose Victorianism that Lagos and his friends in Abuja have saddled him with.

To be cultured and cosmopolitan—at least among the informed—now in the West is to have an eclectic cultural capital and a polyvalent scope of reference that could accommodate Bach and Salawa Abeni, Beethoven and Comfort Omoge, caviar and ikokore, merlot and burukutu, and not to see one as inferior to the other; it is to be equally culturally competent in the Nigeria of Rolls Royces and Cadillacs and the Nigeria of the Agatu yam farmer; it is to be able to move effortlessly from lunch at Golden Gate in Ikoyi to dinner at Mama Put in Obalende; it is to understand that if you look for "Orere Elejigbo," that Yoruba classic by the Lijadu Sisters on YouTube, you'll see an extended version of it being performed in Tel Aviv by Idan K & the Movement of Rhythm, an Israeli band. When a Jew sings "Orere Elejigbo" in Tel Aviv, renders it in Afrobeat because he appreciates the bucolic power of that song, what does that make him? It makes him an "ara oke": the new location of global cultures!

A Race through Race in Missouri

ontrary to popular opinion, race is not always the elephant in the room in America. Sometimes, it is just a three-hundred-pound gorilla in a car. Dateline: Spring 2008. Professor Abdulrasheed Na'Allah, now vice chancellor of Kwara State University, was convener and host of that year's annual meeting of the African Literature Association in his former base at Western Illinois University, Macomb. America is famous for her middle-of-nowhere backyard villages where the local who makes a rare thirty-mile road trip to the next village to buy Budweiser at a cheaper rate claims to have traveled to the end of the world. Throw a university into one such out-of-civilization American backwater, and it acquires the chieftaincy title of "college town." Macomb is one such village, sorry, college town.

How to get to Macomb? No problem, said the poet, Obi Nwakanma, who was then based in St. Louis, Missouri. You just fly to St. Louis. Remi Raji will join us from Ibadan, and we will have a grand reunion before driving out to Macomb. Overestimating his knowledge of the geography of the area like every self-respecting US-based Nigerian writer of my generation, Ogbuefi Nwakanma boasted that Macomb was just a two or three-hour drive from St. Louis. We would rent a car, and all three of us would drive to Macomb. Cakewalk!

I flew happily from Ottawa to St. Louis for the grand reunion with Obi and Remi Raji. Two Nigerian writers under Obi Nwakanma's roof in Missouri—all from the Lagos-Ibadan 1980s–1990s axis of Nigerian letters! The reunion was Nigerianly riotous! We got our beering right. Poundo, egusi, orisirisi. More beering. The day wore on. More beering. Stories and stories and stories of our Ibadan years. More beering, more pepper soup. The day wore on. Obi kept reassuring us that the trip was nothing. We would be in Macomb in no time.

We finally set out around 4 p.m. in the evening, hoping to be in Macomb by 7 p.m. or thereabouts. For the trip, Obi had rented a capitalist car befitting our status. After all, we were three university lecturers. The capitalism of the car, however, excluded GPS. And we did not do MapQuest because Obi was certain he knew the way to Macomb. One hour into the journey, it started to look like we were lost. Two hours into the journey, it started to feel like we were lost.

Getting lost was not a problem. There were three of us with plenty of reunion stories, and we didn't mind the drive. Where we got lost was the problem. I still don't know how, without really saying it, all three of us quietly crept into consciousness of where we were lost; consciousness of that, in the part of America where we were, three black males appearing lost in town could be bad news. We were driving through very small villages. Your one church, one post office, one pub, one elementary school, one grocery store, one gas station, one local mechanic shop village where there are more American flags than there are people. The only police station in such a village is manned by that avuncular sheriff who descends from generations of law enforcement. The type whose great-grandfather was the village's first police officer and whose grandfather was the second police officer and whose father was the third police officer. He is now helped by a second uniformed officer in his twenties. If you bet that folks looking like us don't usually pass through such villages, you probably won't lose the bet.

I stand at six feet and two inches tall, all black male of me. Remi Raji is also a six footer. Obi Nwakanma, our driver, was in his dreadlock days. One Igbotic accent, two Yoru-amala accents. That was a very bad combination driving a very nice car through that type of America. What if a cop pulled us over as was bound to happen at some point?

By now, we had a fourth uninvited passenger in that car that was making us so self-conscious: the gorilla, America's three hundred-pound gorilla. At some point, we were going to have to get gas. The girl at the gas station convenience store couldn't have been more than twenty years old. It was now past 8 p.m. We weighed our options: now you got your gas but does it make sense for all three of you to crowd in on her in the store at this hour of the evening in this middle-of-nowhere village?

Well, we needed to pick up beef jerky, chewing gum, coffee. We needed to pee badly. We entered the store, all three of us, wearing exaggerated smiles and greeting her very warmly. The Nigerian accents disappeared, magically replaced by melodious Americana slithering out beautifully through our noses. As we shopped, we maintained the charm, dropping unnecessary and unsolicited information that we were writers and university people on our way to a prestigious conference in Illinois. It was obvious that we were trying a little too hard not to look the type, not to sound the type, not to be the type. The type? Oh, the dangerous, threatening black male that has been constructed to haunt white imaginations in America for more than three hundred years. If this gas station attendant felt threatened just by our presence in this American village and called the cops, what would they see? Would they see the poetry, the literature, the university in us? Or would they see three threats in a car too nice for them?

I think we decided unconsciously that poetry, literature, and the university are no match for police guns wielded by prejudice. Hence, we behaved. We kept the girl laughing with banter and conversation unconsciously designed to make us sound nonthreatening. We charmed her till we finished our business and drove off. Somehow, we were never stopped, never pulled over . . . in Missouri.

It was almost 11 p.m. when we finally made it to Macomb. As we swished past a gas station, trying to make our way to our hotel, blue and red lights finally flashed behind us.

Obi pulled over. And we waited.

PART THREE

Variations on Love and Self

Dowry

Managing Africa's Many Lovers

'd like to thank the African Studies Course Union of the University of Toronto for the honor of being asked to deliver the keynote lecture at your annual conference. Special thanks are due to Ms. Lili Nkunzimana, president of the ASCU, for her solicitude and the impeccable efficiency with which she organized my trip here today. Her last name tells me she is Francophone so I can comfortably say in my other language, *Mademoiselle Lili, merci beaucoup. Je vous en sais gré!*

Perhaps it is completely fortuitous. Maybe the quiet hands of some benevolent ancestors willed it, designed it to happen this way. But I'm sure it has not escaped any of you that you have asked me to reflect on Africa and the Black Diaspora today, February 15, merely a day after the entire world celebrated the feast of love known as Valentine's Day. No, I am not grumbling that you deprived me the opportunity of attending to matters of the heart yesterday as I had to spend Valentine's Day revising and cleaning up this lecture instead of buying roses and making arrangements for a candlelit dinner in a cozy, chandeliered environment.

Anyway, I am not complaining. I am just drawing your attention to the uncanny

---

Keynote lecture delivered at the annual conference of the African Studies Course Union, University of Toronto, February 15, 2013 coincidence that I am delivering a lecture about love and lovers—Africa's surfeit of lovers and the implications of that love affair for the Black Diaspora—only a day after the feast of love. Because I am a Nigerian and we are usually accused by the rest of Africa of being dominant and having a tendency to suck the oxygen out of the room, I am going to tell you proudly and boastfully that we have only just won the African Cup of Nations, the continent's most prestigious soccer competition, and are therefore enjoying our moment as the continent's beautiful bride within an overall atmospherics of continental love.[3] That moment too gels nicely with the theme of the present discourse: love.

If you are still wondering what love's got to do with it (apologies to Swiss singer, Tina Turner), a look at the title of this lecture would convince you that we are here to reflect on and share the love, for he who talks dowry talks about transactions and imaginaries of love, about matters of the heart, and about a particular mode of translating that human arrangement into culturally sanctioned nuptials in certain cultures. Dowry in Africa? Those of you with an ear for nuance and distinction ought to be worried by now. Isn't dowry mainly a Southeast Asian, especially Indian, affair? Does this professor know what he is talking about?

I do. Although dowry is very often used whenever the speaker means bride-price in many of the "Englishes" you hear in sub-Saharan Africa, that is not what is happening here. I have not fallen prey to that commonplace confusion. I am talking about dowry—money, goods, or estate that a woman brings to her husband at marriage—because that, precisely, has been the mode of Africa's transactions with the throngs of suitors, fiancés, and lovers that fate, history, and oftentimes, self-inflicted vulnerabilities, have thrown across her path in the last five hundred years and counting.

Indeed, it is safe to say that no continent has enjoyed more professions of love than Africa in all of human history. I don't make this sweeping assertion lightly. In other continents, the conquered were very often spared the nicety and the hypocrisy of pretense. For instance, I am not aware that the European hardened criminals, condemned prisoners, and nut cases who would become the nemesis of the Aborigines in Australia went there professing love for anything or anybody other than themselves. Similarly, the European conquerors of the Americas made little or no profession of love for those whose lands they seized. Didn't Friar

---

3. The reference is to the African Cup of Nations soccer competition which Nigeria won on February 10, 2013, just five days before this lecture was delivered.

Bartolomé de Las Casas (1552/1992), that tireless chronicler of the Americas who wrote *A Short Account of the Destruction of the Indies,* inform us that Hatuey, a famous Indian chief from the island of Hispaniola, declared before he was burned by the Spaniards that he would rather go to hell if heaven was where the European Christian conquerors of the Americas went? There is definitely no love lost between the violated owner of the land and the European immigrant in this picture. The more than five hundred pages of *Hernán Cortés: Letters from Mexico,* translated and edited by Anthony Pagden (1971), are a veritable testimony to this absence of love, pretext, and hypocrisy between conqueror and conquered in America.

The scenario was slightly different in Africa. The land and people were fictioned as a receptive female subject to be taken, penetrated, and had, in the imaginaries of Europeans driven to encounter the Other by the curiosities unleashed by the spirit of the Enlightenment. The dominant idiom of this taking, this penetrating, this having, was love. I am not so sure, for instance, that King Mutesa of Buganda shares Hatuey's hostile feeling toward Europeans when he encounters Europe, at least not if we are to believe one of the most memorable fictional refractions of that historical encounter between African and European. I am talking about David Rubadiri's (2004) great poem, "Stanley Meets Mutesa." Permit me to cite the powerful last line of the poem:

And the West is let in.

Before the West is let in, Rubadiri's King Mutesa had famously uttered the words, "White man, you are welcome"! Love, my friends, is in the air. In Africa, nobody is hurrying to hell to avoid contact with European Christians in heaven. If you are wondering why love is in the air, you have to consider the entire modes of discourse which preceded and framed this encounter. For such a framing of the politics of encounter, let us go to Cardinal Verdier, archbishop of Paris in the heyday of empire and a staunch opponent of fascism. Describing World War II as a "crusade," Cardinal Verdier (1940) enthused that "we are struggling to preserve the freedom of people throughout the world, whether they be great or small peoples, and to preserve their possessions and their very lives. No other war has had aims that are more spiritual, moral, and, in sum, more Christian." Now, this is all very beautiful. You can't possibly fault these sentiments. The problem begins once Cardinal Verdier thinks beyond the platitude that he calls "peoples." Once he logs into more specific referents such as color and geography, his humanism takes on the dimension of ecstatic love, hence this famous statement of his about the project of love that was the civilizing mission of France in Africa:

> Nothing is more moving than this gesture of the Frenchman, taking his black brother by the hand and helping him to rise. This hierarchic but nonetheless black collaboration, this fraternal love stooping toward the blacks to measure their possibilities of thinking and feeling . . . this art, in a word, of helping them progress through wise development of their personality toward an improved physical, social and moral well-being; this is how France's colonizing mission on the black continent appears to us. (Verdier, 1939)

Although the Roman Catholic cardinal was talking about fraternal love in his framing of French colonialism and the subsequent régimes of coloniality it spawned, history teaches us that Africa was the object of all the manifestations of that intense human emotion throughout her history of encounter with conquerors. Name any kind of love—fraternal, agape, carnal—and you are sure to encounter a very rich cast of characters, sallying forth from their European homelands in waves after the Portuguese blazed the trail in the fifteenth century, for picaresque adventures of love in Africa. So, in a way, Wole Soyinka is only partially right to have insisted in his latest book, *Of Africa,* that Africa possesses one unremarked distinction of having not been the subject of claims of discovery like the Americas or Australasia. Writes Soyinka (2012):

> No one actually claims to have "discovered" Africa. Neither the continent as an entity nor indeed any of her later offspring—the modern states—celebrates the equivalent of America's Columbus Day. This gives it a self-constitutive identity, an unstated autochthony that is denied other continents and subcontinents. The narrative history of encounters with Africa does not dispute with others or revise itself over the "discovery" of Africa. . . . Africa appears to have been "known about," speculated over, explored both in actuality and fantasy, even mapped—Greeks, Jews, Arabs, Phoenicians, etc., took their turns—but no narrative has come down to us that actually lays personal or racial claim to the discovery of the continent.

I say Soyinka is only partially right because Africa has a second distinction that even the Nobel laureate appears not to have noticed. She is the only continent whose modes of encounter with and insertion into modernity were fictioned almost exclusively through registers of love by those with a superior capacity to narrativize and globalize those love stories. Let me emphasize this point: Africa is humanity's only labor of love. No greater love hath the Arab invader, the European explorer, slaver, colonizer, missionary, captain of industry, corporate CEO, multinational corporation CEO, humanitarian aid worker, Christian charity worker, NGO worker, foreign development expert, expatriate, Hollywood celebrity serial child adopter; no greater love hath all these characters for Africa that they gave up the comforts of Arabia and Europe and came to risk mosquitoes and malaria in the heart of darkness. Even this imperative of love accounted for the obduracy of Margaret Thatcher and Ronald Reagan on the question of sanctions against apartheid South Africa in the 1980s. So great was their love for Black South Africans that these two leaders of the free world opposed sanctions against the apartheid state for fear that their beloved Blacks would suffer disproportionately.

These lovers introduced dowry as the only mode of transaction with the beautiful bride on whose account they traveled. Africa has been paying this dowry to her numerous lovers in the last five hundred years of her history. She has paid in cash and kind. She has paid dowries of land and territory to these lovers; she has paid dowries of copper, gold, diamonds, cocoa, coffee, rubber, ivory, coltan, uranium, crude oil. Africa is the bride fated to pay expensive dowries to lovers and fiancés who do not mind polyandry. Never mind the rivalry between today's princes charming—America, Europe, China—seeking Africa's hand in marriage. So long as the dowry payments continue to flow from Africa, these guys don't mind polyandry. Sometimes, Africa's dowry payment has a name, a face, black flesh, and red blood. Patrice Lumumba was dowry and so were Eduardo Mondlane, Steve Biko, and Thomas Sankara.

Other times, the dowry is neither quantifiable nor measurable because it operates mostly as emotional jouissance for the career lover of Africa. The humanitarian aid worker, the Christian charity worker, the NGO development volunteer, the Hollywood celebrity serial child adopter (Madonna), all kinds of organizations without borders, Bono, Jeffrey Sachs, and Angelina Jolie are all career lovers of the continent functioning within a mechanism I have referred to in previous lectures and essays as the Mercy Industrial Complex. This category of Africa's lovers does not demand the sort of dowry exacted by the colonizer or the CEOs of Shell Petroleum, Halliburton, and Siemens. Their dowry lies in the unmappable emotional satisfaction of the messianic complex. Another child adopted away from the poverty of mealie in Malawi offers more than an occasion for media razzmatazz. To the

Hollywood celebrity serial child adopter, the gesture offers the psychic satisfaction of the hand that giveth.

Other times still, the dowry régime has yielded consequences that have altered the course of history forever. The lover of Africa who was a slaver carried his human dowry across the Atlantic for more than three hundred years. At the purely economic level, Eric Williams (1944) assures us in his monumentally important book, *Capitalism and Slavery,* that the labor of that human dowry paid by Africa informed the complexion of capitalism as we came to know it. In other words, Africa's dowry produced a Black Diaspora in such a way as to profoundly inflect the topography of wealth creation and accumulation in the West.

Now, this is where this dowry business really gets interesting. We know that to create a diaspora is to create novel cultural lifeworlds, new imaginaries, new modes of being and apprehension, new modalities of sentience that are not just locked in the politics of emplantment in a new world but must also contend with that which cannot be disappeared: home. "That's all it takes really, pressure, and time," says Red in one of my favorite films of all times, *The Shawshank Redemption* (1994). Pressure and time may dissolve the concrete geographical essence of home for the diaspora population, but they never really empty it of psychic content, symbolic force, and matricial value. They never empty it of its capacity to mobilize and interpellate the diaspora population affectively in terms of articulations of identity. This explains why registers of tracery and connections underwrite the cultures of the Black Diaspora, of any diaspora: roots and routes, origins, sources, memory, remembering, and re-membering become crucial to a telos of subjectivity that Brent Hayes Edwards (2003) refers to as "the practice of diaspora" in his magnificent book of the same title.

To animate the emotion of "home" or "source" despite the wear and tear placed on memory by pressure and time, to articulate modes of being in the present nurtured by the political and philosophical resonances of origins involves a scrutiny of the transaction between the self-professed lover of Africa and the dowry-paying bride. This query is an epistemological obligation for the Black Diaspora population. Was dowry taken at gunpoint by a lover who would accept it only in human form capable of working on his plantations in the Americas, or did Africa, the mesmerized bride, offer that dowry too quickly and too enthusiastically, carried away by gifts of rum, mirrors, and other industrial products dangled before her by the lover from across the seas?

The answers which various generations of Black Diaspora intellectuals have found for these questions have had profound implications for the genre of self-fashioning and self-writing known as the return narrative. If you look at a certain Black radical tradition of home and memory, which encompasses the divergent and disparate intellection and praxes of, say, W. E. B Du Bois, Marcus Garvey, Bob Marley, Aimé Césaire, Léon-Gontran Damas, and Molefi Kete Asante, you will encounter imaginaries of Africa and return narratives which devolve from what appears to be a clear conviction that Europe exacted that dowry at gunpoint. It is not for nothing that Bob Marley's Buffalo soldiers were "stolen from Africa," not sold in Africa by Africans. And we know who Bob Marley is accusing of theft. No text articulates this position better than Césaire's (1955/2007) slim but powerful book, *Discourse on Colonialism.* For Césaire, the dowry was forcibly taken not just by Europe but also by the particular kind of Europe that the other encountered: a Europe that was at her most rapaciously and brutally capitalistic.

There is a second model associated notably with the Henry Louis Gates (1999) of the *Wonders of the African World* fame. I call it the dirty linen model. This model somewhat shifts the responsibility for slavery from the lover of Africa who went in search of slaves to the beautiful bride, Africa, who is deemed to have been too eager to offer the dowry. This model, obviously, has spawned more problematic imaginaries of Africa in the Diasporic imagination. Lingering resentment of the home that sold you—if that is how you elect to see it—into slavery hardly allows for the romanticized memory-making of the first tradition. When Léon-Gontran Damas, one of the three founding fathers of Négritude, sings, "give me back my black dolls / so that I may play with them / the naïve games of my instinct," I don't think Henry Louis Gates would supply any chorus to that song. Rather, I imagine him quipping: "Pray, Monsieur Damas, how did your black dolls get to the Americas in the first place?"

Despites these tensions, something unites these two modes of diasporic engagement of Africa and that is the desire to make Africa mean, to make her fundamentally mean something. Whether you are claiming Africa radically, romanticizing her, and longing for the day that your soul shall make the return journey to Guinée, like the character, Médouze, does in Euzhan Palcy's (1983) film, *Sugar Cane Alley;* whether you are probing history and memory in order to establish what you call Africa's complicity in and responsibility for slavery, as is the case with Henry Louis Gates and those of his persuasion, you are involved, as a Black Diasporic subject, in a quest for meaning marked by an initial anxiety of contact. The anxiety here is not akin to the "silence of assessment" that brokered the encounter between Stanley and Mutesa. Rather, this is an anxiety spawned and fed by the fear and the undecidabilities of the unknown. She has been gone for more than three hundred years, this Black Diasporic sister. Africa is now a narrative to her, and she is apprehensive of what this narrative might portend. In a keynote lecture I delivered to the annual conference of the Stanford Forum for African Studies at Stanford University last year, I tried to map this anxiety using the example of Richard Wright.[4]

The anxiety of contact, the fear of the unknown, which makes a dumfounded Richard Wright exclaim "Africa?" on hearing a suggestion that he should travel to Africa, is also at the root of the torn and divided consciousness which runs through Countee Cullen's (1925) famous poem, "Heritage." The poem speaks for itself, and we need not remind ourselves of more than its first interrogatory line here:

What is Africa to me?

The business of remembering and re-membering the schism in the world of the Diasporic sons and daughters of Africa often involves, among other gestures of reconnection, symbolic voyages to Africa to visit the sites of memory. Those voyages to the Atlantic slave coast of Africa, those emotional narratives about returnee sons and daughters breaking down in tears in Gorée, Elmina, Cape Coast, and Badagry, are all part of a multilayered ritual of reconnection and re-membering. There is, however, a problem with this mode of reentry. If you explore the wealth of documentaries and literature of reentry, if you examine even anecdotal accounts that one collects in encounters with members of the Black Diaspora community, you will discover that the Africa that is most sought after is largely a synchronic one, imagined as ancestral, fixed in her past and ancient grandness.

Irrespective of the actualities of the continent, Africa is where you go to find your history. Lagos, Accra, Dakar, Bamako, and Luanda are just locations of passage, intrusions, or distractions that you must deal with before your grand encounter with the sites of memory. On arrival from the United States, from Canada, from the Caribbean, Africa's capital cities offer you an airport and a hotel to spend the night and prepare your trip to the real Africa—the Africa that is history, the Africa that is memory, the Africa that is ancient. You hardly have time to notice or connect with the postmodern whirl of the city around you. You are in a hurry to get to sites

---

4. See essay, "Capitalism and Memory," in this book.

of psychic communion with Kunta Kinte and Olaudah Equiano. You are more interested in Kumbi Saleh than Accra. Askia the Great and Mansa Kankan Musa speak to you more than Ellen Johnson Sirleaf[5] and other contemporary leaders of the continent. The African Union and NEPAD are ancient Greek to you. You are looking for slave forts and slave routes, and you don't want Africa's present all around you to get in the way.

What accounts for this apparent fixation with the part of Africa that is historic as opposed to her actualities and contemporaneous vistas of meaning in the Diasporic imagination? Does this harbor a desire to reconnect with Africa precisely at the point at which one left in the sixteenth century? I think something deeper is going on, and it is related to the postcolonial forms of dowry that Africa is paying to a nebulous lover we shall describe as Western desire, for want of a better descriptor. I am talking about the desire which Chinua Achebe famously describes in his Conrad essay, "An Image of Africa." Writes Achebe (1977):

> Quite simply it is the desire—one might indeed say the need—in Western psychology to set Africa up as a foil to Europe, as a place of negations at once remote and vaguely familiar, in comparison with which Europe's own state of spiritual grace will be manifest.

The dowry of the image or the dowry of the single story—apologies to Chimamanda Adichie—is what Africa now pays to this lover, Western desire. Now, this is a much more powerful lover, with considerable technologies of dissemination.

With considerable impunity, this lover takes only the single story of poverty, hunger, and disease and broadcasts it in Western imagination as Africa's present. Mr. Western Desire singlehandedly determines what he wants to consume of Africa. A budding American scholar of African literatures and cultures, Mr. David Mastey, is currently working on a doctoral dissertation on the privileging and consumption of African child soldier narratives in the United States. Mr. Mastey is working under my supervision, and I am learning a lot from his work and inquiry into the hunger for African child soldier stories by the American public. There is a desire for the single story of trauma and vulnerability, and Africa pays that dowry willy-nilly. It doesn't even matter whether what is at issue concerns Africa or not; she is the continent that must keep on giving a singular idea of herself to feed Western desire.

---

5. President of the Republic of Liberia and Africa's first female president.

Witness Gail Collins (2013), a columnist for the *New York Times,* assessing the Lance Armstrong tragedy in a January edition of her column:

> There's always a chance. Armstrong could demonstrate his remorse by dedicating the rest of his life to fighting rural poverty in an extremely remote section of Africa, preferably one where residents are limited to a quart of water a day. His fans would come flocking back, although Armstrong would hardly notice because the critical part of the deal would be staying in Niger or Burkina Faso forever.

Now, how did this columnist make the leap from Lance Armstrong to the idea of rural poverty in Africa? You could essay the explanation that deep in her subconscious lies the idea of Africa as a site of redemption for Western rejects and abjects but that would be cold comfort. It doesn't account for the reflex. That reference is gratuitous and silly but such, often, is the first point of contact with what is constructed as Africa's present for her sons and daughters in the Diaspora. Everywhere the Black Canadian or the African American turns to in terms of the imagery of Africa that is fed into the Western imagination and consciousness, they encounter a depressing tableau of abjection, trauma, and tragedy. Africa's past, recycled and romanticized in robust traditions of Black intellection and identity-making, comes to represent—at least in the Diasporic imagination—a safe haven from the monolithically constructed ugliness of the continent's present.

If you are an African American or a Black Canadian beginning to take a very serious interest in Africa, Gail Collins just made Niger and Burkina Faso very unpalatable for you. If your interest in Africa survives your encounter with Collins's column, chances are you would prefer Négritude's Africa of beautiful bucolic black dolls of the ancient times to Collins's Africa of contemporary misery. And if you persist in tracing your origin, it is unlikely now you will claim to have discovered that your ancestors came from Burkina Faso or Niger. I wouldn't blame you if you rigged things in favor of Botswana or Ghana.

Sometimes, the single story of the African present comes from her own sons and daughters in the Diaspora. Witness the damage done by Keith Richburg in his 1997 book, *Out of America: A Black Man Confronts Africa.* This is one angry Black man who spent years covering some of the continent's most brutal conflicts for the *Washington Post* and arrived at the conclusion that he is extremely lucky that those African savages sold his ancestors into slavery. At least they are now Americans and have escaped Africa's horrendous present. Make no mistake about this, I may grumble about Mr. Richburg's book, but I do perfectly understand where he is coming from. In fact, a Nigerian is not in the position to grumble too loudly about Mr. Richburg. To grumble too much is to elicit the question: so what have you guys made of fifty years of the Nigerian present? Have you not produced your own brood of postcolonial Black Nigerian lovers of Nigeria who are now exacting dowry from the Nigerian people, leaving them in unbelievable poverty and corruption even with so much oil wealth? If you look too closely at Nigeria's present as it has been produced since 1999 by one of Africa's most corrupt ruling elite, it is not too difficult to understand why a Black Diasporic subject may want to have nothing to do with the African present.

The responsibility of Africa's ruling class in producing a present that could be so unpalatable for our Black Diasporic cousins aside, what does Africa try to do about this postmodern dowry of the singular image that she keeps paying to the much more determined lover that is Western desire? How does she struggle to get past the impunity of gratuitous negative referencing as exemplified by Gail Collins? Africa could offer counter-narratives into which the Black Diaspora could plug for glimpses of a present much richer than what the single stories present. Despite the nightmare that is her ruling elite, this is what my country, Nigeria, has achieved for instance with the phenomenon that is Nollywood. Out of postcolonial lack, Nigeria has given world culture Nollywood, the world's second largest movie industry. Nollywood movies are not just immensely popular across Africa, they constitute a new cultural bridge between Africa and her Diaspora. In Canada, in the United States, and across the Caribbean, Nollywood offers counter-narratives of the African present to the Black Diaspora.

Sometimes the counter-narrative of the present comes in the shape of youth culture and agency. The Azonto dance, for instance, originates from Ghana, sweeps through the rest of the continent, especially Nigeria, and has become a cultural connecting point with the continent for young Black and African Diasporans in the West. I mention Nollywood and Azonto because Africans, hung up on science and technology, often underestimate the power of culture to globalize every area of their genius, including their technological innovations. There is no better narrative of the Japanese people—and her technology—than the statement that sushi makes on Western and non-Western palates alike. Never underestimate what Gangnam style is doing for the South Korean brand on the global stage. Who in the West is developing a taste for Korean cars and technology after encountering Korea through Gangnam style? That is what culture has the potential and capacity to do.

The bitter truth, however, is that counter-narratives of the African present function in asymmetrical power relations with narratives of impunity which insist on Africa as a single story. Nollywood may have made inroads in Canada, for instance, and may have even gone beyond the Black Canadian community since Nollywood movies are now often represented in Canadian film festivals; all it takes to roll back the gains is one powerful Canadian single story about Africa. Consider something as simple as language. The linguistic diversity of Nigeria, Ghana, and other African countries is shown even through the deployment of various Englishes in Nollywood. Then one Canadian novel is published. This novel talks about language but constantly hints at "dialects." For the perceptive reader, language comes across as an intrusion into a world of dialects. Language is only comfortable in its world whenever the plot shifts to Canada. Then this Canadian novel goes ahead and wins the 2012 Scotia Bank Giller Prize, by far, Canada's most prestigious literary prize.

That novel is *419* by Will Ferguson (2012). Mr. Ferguson is a travel writer. He has traveled extensively and published four travel books. He did not travel to Nigeria or Africa to research his novel. Africa is the place you can represent with impunity, especially if you have expatriate friends in Africa who "know" the culture. Says Mr. Ferguson:

> I was fortunate to have several superb early readers who provided insights, advice, and corrections: Kirsten Olson; Jacqueline Ford, who has traveled extensively in the francophone region of West Africa; Kathy Robson, who has lived and worked in Nigeria; and Helen Chatburn-Ojehomon, who is married to a Nigerian citizen and working in Ibadan, north of Lagos. Many thanks to all of them for the feedback! The depictions of Nigerian culture and customs are solely my responsibility. . . . Helen and Kathy in particular gave me excellent advice on the English spoken in Nigeria but in the end I found the richness of the dialect too difficult to capture on the page. Instead, I added only the slightest touch, to give readers just a hint of the full flavor.

I guess it is too much to expect Mr. Ferguson to go to Nigeria for this gigantic project instead of relying on a handful of expatriates for expertise on "Nigerian culture and customs?" There is mention of more sources on his website, but I found none when I visited it. Well, let us examine the quality of the expertise offered Mr. Ferguson by his expatriate knowers of Nigerian culture and customs. No Nigerian would read this howler on page 117 by the omniscient narrator—with strong hints of authorial intrusion—without risking a heart attack: "*Egobia* was from the Yoruba language, the language Winston spoke with his grandparents. *Ego* meant 'money,' and *bia* meant 'come to me,' making Egobia more an incantation than an actual name. '*Money come*'" (Ferguson, 2012, p.117).

The mislabeling of two Igbo words as Yoruba is not a one-time occurrence in the novel. Make no mistake about the gravity of this howler. There is a Sergeant Brisebois in the novel. As Canadian readers of the novel, this is the equivalent of your being told by the narrator that the last name, Brisebois, is from two Anglo-Canadian words, "briser" and "bois." Imagine what the French people of Quebec would have thought of Mr. Ferguson if this had happened. Sadly, there are more howlers in the novel. Of the January 1966 coup, Mr. Ferguson's omniscient narrator informs his Canadian readers that this was "the same coup that left Nigeria's prime minister dead and the regional premiers rounded up and imprisoned." I wonder who, among his "superb early readers," told Mr. Ferguson that Samuel Ladoke Akintola, the premier of the western region, was rounded up and imprisoned? Somehow, none of Mr. Ferguson's expatriate experts of Nigerian "culture and customs," none of his editors at Viking Canada, none of the judges of the Giller Prize caught any of these howlers. I wager that Mr. Ferguson could very well have written that "Ego" and "bia" are two Gikuyu, Swahili, or Lingala words, and nobody would have noticed. In Africa, we are interchangeable.

Yet this is the canonized cultural artifact, an award-winning novel, which will shape Nigeria and Africa in the Canadian imagination, carrying the imprimatur of the Giller Prize and the considerable capital that comes with it, in the foreseeable future. Can Nollywood as a counter-narrative stack up to a novel that has won the Giller Prize in Canada? No matter how well-spoken Nollywood star actors and actresses such as Desmond Elliot, Ramsey Nouah, and Genevieve Nnaji are, they and their ilk are now fixed for Canadian cultural consumption as a bunch of dialect-speaking Africans.

When a Black Canadian picks up this novel and encounters "Nigerian culture and customs" described by a powerful Canadian writer relying mostly on the second-hand accounts of his expatriate friends, would this Black Canadian wonder if Mr. Ferguson would not have spent months in France immersing himself in the culture and the language of that country if he was writing a novel about France? Would this Black Canadian want to move beyond this novel to ascertain that the cybercrime 419 is not Nigeria's greatest innovation as Mr. Ferguson claims? And, most importantly, would the Black Canadian understand that the Nigeria trapped in the 399 pages of this prize-winning Canadian novel is yet another dowry paid by Africa to one of her lovers in 2012?

Caribbean Self, African Selfie

bring you warm greetings from Accra, Ghana, where I am currently based. I understand that winter has been particularly brutal this year. You could use some of the warmth I brought from Africa in my hand luggage. I am told by the organizers of this event—to whom I owe immense debts of gratitude for inviting me to deliver this keynote lecture—that "loud and proud" is the theme of your Caribbean-Africa Connections week this year. In other words, the Caribbean and African Association of the University of British Columbia has decided to scream the cultures of Africa and the Caribbean from the rooftops this week. You want to proudly highlight what connects Africa and the Caribbean in the arena of culture—and in defiance of the Atlantic Ocean. You want to inscribe your so-called otherness loudly and proudly on this beautiful campus of UBC. When I thought about your theme on receiving the invitation for this lecture, it evoked a sense of drama. How do you proclaim Caribbean and African connections "loud and proud" without being dramatic? I have therefore taken the unusual route of plotting this

Keynote lecture delivered at the inauguration of the Connections Week of the Caribbean and African Association of the University of British Columbia, Vancouver, Canada, March 10, 2014 lecture as a one-act play in five scenes. At any rate, on my way here from Accra, I did get into some drama in London . . .

Act One, Scene One

Date: March 6, 2014. Location: Terminal Three, London Heathrow Airport. Mission: awaiting an Air Canada connecting flight to Ottawa en route to Vancouver for this lecture. I was coming from back-to-back keynote lectures in Johannesburg, Pretoria, Accra, and Lagos. Although I was jetlagged and tired, I already had a draft of this lecture in the bag. Nevertheless, there was something I wasn't quite satisfied about. I was trying to look at the Caribbean-African thing beyond the routine of memory. Must the ties that bind always be about memory? I wasn't sure that what I had in the first draft had satisfactorily answered that question. I had seven hours to kill at Heathrow. I decided to shell out sixty pounds to rent a room and shower cubicle for three hours in one of the "capitalist" lounges of the airport. I needed that space and time to continue my reflection on what lies—or what ought to lie—beyond the horizon of memory-making and memory-reliving whenever Africa and the Caribbean actuate a handshake across the Atlantic.

In essence, I did not need anything or anybody to remind me of how memory ties the Caribbean and other parts of the Black Diaspora to Africa. I wanted to move conceptually beyond that paradigm. As I moved wearily through the familiar mass of fatigued bodies dragging a cornucopia of hand luggage through the malls of Heathrow, making my way to the F Lounge, I bumped into just the one thing I wanted to avoid: memory. It came in the exact body shape, height, skin tone, facial features, and even dressing style of Professor Ato Quayson. I am sure you all know Professor Quayson? If you don't know him, you have a very urgent problem that only Google can help you resolve.

In the engaging business of theorizing Africa and her Diaspora in academe, Professor Quayson has been one of my formidable mentors in the last decade and a half. I had not seen him since the African Literature Association's meeting in Dallas in 2012. I'd been to his University of Toronto base to deliver lectures on occasion, but he'd always been out of town. And there he was before me, like an apparition, in a crowded airport lounge in London. I screamed and grabbed him in a hug that certainly wasn't a bear hug. Loads of back patting. Deft feet movement and shuffling that you could call some kind of esoteric dance. Strings of jazzed up sentences delivered in a mishmash of English, Pidgin, and West African slang intrusions. These happened in seconds.

In other words, I was performing, right there in the open in London, an unscripted and impromptu reunion ritual which I somehow expected Ato Quayson or any other African brother to connect with and respond to appropriately. "I'm not Ato," screamed the bemused figure in my arms, struggling to set himself free from my Black hug while laughing in bemused acknowledgment of the accompanying semi-dance rituals. Remember, all this was happening within seconds, a succession of quick-paced actions and events. I realized to my utter embarrassment that I had grabbed the wrong man! The guy I grabbed and held in such a warm embrace was not Ato Quayson, just his Siamese look-alike!

I was going to start apologizing profusely when my "victim," very friendly but obviously relieved to be released from my grip, assured me that no apology was necessary. In fact, he was very intrigued by my enactments of recognition and the effusive ritual of warmth I enacted when I thought he was Ato Quayson. According to him, everything about that instinctive, unplanned, impromptu but ritualized performance was also native to him. He would have done exactly the same thing in my shoes, he reassured me.

"And where are you from?" I asked. "Trinidad," came his swift response. At this point, ladies and gentlemen, I knew I had to offer the brother a beer. I mean, here was my Nigerian self, thinking it was engaging Ato Quayson's Ghanaian self in ritualized modes of African warmth and connection only for those cultural enactments to be claimed by a Trinidadian also seeing himself, his people, his culture, his story, and his memory in those moves. On my way to an airport lounge to think beyond culture and memory in terms of how best to reconceptualize African and Caribbean modes of engagement, culture and memory beckon, saying, "Ogbeni Pius, we're not done yet!"

Act One, Scene Two

Maybe I should have known that memory and culture wouldn't lend themselves to the easy glossing over I was going to do at that airport lounge before I received a Trinidadian jolt of reality. After all, another place, another time, memory and culture had served me notice of their power of persistence in any evocation of the linkages between the Caribbean and Africa. That other place is none other than this lovely city of Vancouver in this beautiful Canadian province of British Columbia. That other time was the 1990s when I pursued my doctoral degree right here in this very university.

Back in those hectic days of doctoral work, some of us needed the occasional escape from the cast of French poststructuralist thinkers who, in the hands of North American academics, had turned postcolonial and postmodernist theory into an obscurantist terror machine. In a good week, your migraine was limited to struggling to blend the impenetrable prose of Judith Butler, Gayatri Spivak, and Homi Bhabha into a deconstructive paradigm for the novels and cultures of Africa and the Caribbean. In a bad week, you had to add Jacques Lacan, Louis Althusser, Michel Foucault, Jean Baudrillard, Jacques Derrida, Julia Kristeva, Helene Cixous, Luce Irigaray, and so many other usual and unusual French suspects to that mix.

To reinforce that overdose of high theory, you were required on occasion to rent a few names from the Frankfurt school of theory. You completed this theoretical cocktail, which left African and Caribbean novels struggling for oxygen, with Antonio Gramsci and a necessary throwback to Karl Marx. In preparing one's theoretical paradigm for African and Caribbean fiction, one often felt like Getafix the Druid preparing the magic potion for Asterix and Obelix. We threw so many names into the pot of that theoretical magic potion. Trust me, ladies and gentlemen, when you have spent a week trying to foist Foucault's power/knowledge combo on Chinua Achebe and Mariama Ba or attempting a Derridean deconstruction of Edwige Danticat and Patrick Chamoiseau via *différance*-speak, you needed to unwind desperately. Ah, the good old days of graduate school!

For those of us in the African and Caribbean communities, unwinding twice a week happened ritually in one watering hole: the Anza Club, close to Main and Broadway here in Vancouver. That nightclub was not just the place where we went to booze and do all the wild and unmentionable things that students do in their riotous twenties, just before other realities of life set in, it was also for us some sort of pilgrimage to a location of culture and memory. The Anza was the only nightclub in Vancouver at the time dedicated to African and Caribbean music. We went there to swing to reggae, calypso, zouk, soukouss, makossa, and soca. We went there to subject our waists to rhythms of high life, Afrobeat, juju, and the kora and balafon offerings of the sub-Saharan African Sahel.

Whatever we danced to, the cut was in how we all danced and what we all recognized. Recognition of source and of origins. When the Caribbean students danced, we, their African cousins, would marvel in recognition of rhythms, styles, and movements that took us all the way back to our respective villages in Africa. And when we, Africans, danced, our Caribbean folks remembered. They just remembered. Like the Trinidadian reacting to my reunion rituals at Heathrow, Caribbean students of my day at UBC watched us, Africans, dance at the Anza Club and remembered their respective homes in the Black Atlantic. "Ah, we have this dance in Saint Lucia!," you would hear somebody exclaim if I was enacting variations on the "elele kure" shoulder dance of the Okun people in Kogi State, Nigeria.

Whether it's in the passenger mall of an international airport or on the dance floor of a Vancouver nightclub, the Africa-Caribbean nexus, spelt out in terms of encounters between continental Africans and their cousins in the Black Atlantic, has spawned imaginaries of the self, rooted in memory and culture since the historical moment of separation. If you are from the continent, you frame narratives of source-culturehood around these issues. If you belong in the Black Diaspora, you weave imaginaries of cultural survivorhood around the same issues. What lived, what survived, and how you produced newness from the old become, for you, the loom of identity-making in the present. But, mostly, you remember in order to re-member.

Act One, Scene Three

The literature and discourses of both sides are rich in constructions of the self, rooted in the politics and memory of remembering. For the Caribbean self, return narratives are crucial to the architecture of remembering and re-membering. The business of remembering and re-membering sometimes involves, among other gestures of reconnection, symbolic voyages to Africa to visit the sites of memory. Those voyages to the Atlantic slave coast of Africa, those emotional narratives about returnee sons and daughters breaking down in tears in Gorée, Elmina, Cape Coast, and Badagry, are all part of a multilayered ritual of reconnection. For the Caribbean self and other Black Diasporic selves, the return narrative, especially its twentieth century enactments, was one way of trying to answer the query, "What is Africa to me?" in Countee Cullen's (1925) famous poem "Heritage."

Not all return narratives romanticize Africa like Countee Cullen and our friends in the Négritude movement did. Some, like Henry Louis Gates, belong in the dirty linen school of return narratives. They return to Africa to see the faces of the descendants of the greedy ancestors who sold them to slavery. Their problem is not with the white slaver but with my ancestors who sold their ancestors. One model of return narratives romanticizes Africa and demands reparations from the descendants of the white slaver; another criminalizes Africa and demands an apology from me for the sins of my ancestors who sold their ancestors. However, both models meet at the crossroads of meaning. They share a desire to make Africa mean. The question thus arises: what exactly feeds the impulse of these return narratives on the part of the Black Diaspora and their modes of actuation? Why were return narratives so crucial to the making of the Caribbean self in the twentieth century?

Act One, Scene Four

The answers are myriad and complex, but I think we should focus here on one possible reason why the twentieth century offered us the return narrative as one of the major routes to identity-making by the Caribbean self. Despite disagreements on modes of engaging the continent as source-culture—were we stolen by white slavers or were we sold by our heartless African cousins?—there can be no denying the fact that, before the "mourning" after independence set in, the twentieth century was the moment of Africa's heroism and African heroism. It was the century which saw Africa successfully challenge, undermine, and overcome some five hundred years of truth claims by modernity, five hundred years of placing a question mark on the humanity of Africans and Black people elsewhere. It was the century of political and cultural nationalism, of decolonization, of the anti-apartheid struggle, of coming into peoplehood, of coming into postcolonial statehood.

Indeed, the twentieth century was an extremely auspicious time for Black people all over the world to plug into this African specter of global heroism. Your source-culture was heroic. What is more, the making of this grand narrative of heroism—that is, the challenge to and dismantling of colonialism—was not an isolated enterprise undertaken by continental Africans behind the back of their cousins in the Black Diaspora. In fact, the intellectual, cultural, and political bases of these forms of African heroism were mostly born in the Diaspora and devolved from an organic collaboration between Africa's emergent political, nationalist, and intellectual class and their counterparts from the Black Diaspora.

Pan-Africanism and Négritude are two good examples of the collective contributions of continental Africans and the Black Diaspora to the making of Africa's twentieth century anti-imperialist heroism. A great deal of the intellectual energy that later went into African nationalism was honed in London and Paris in collaborations between the nascent African nationalist class and their counterparts from the Caribbean and Black America. So formidable and far-reaching were these collaborations and joint efforts that two of the most famous theorizers and chroniclers of Africa's twentieth century heroism were from the Black Diaspora. I am thinking here of the Frantz Fanon of *The Wretched of the Earth* and the Walter Rodney of *How Europe Underdeveloped Africa*.

If the pervading sense of having participated in the heroic self-recovery effort of the mother continent was a contributory factor to the flourishing of the return narrative, the principal mode of African heroism in the twentieth century greatly enhanced it. The struggle for cultural and political freedom yielded the persona of the nationalist-statesman as a towering African hero. He was that colorful and charismatic character, that brilliant and powerful orator who became a transcendental African moral and ethical figure (before tragically becoming other unmentionable things in a good number of cases). The magic of this figure made association with Africa as home, memory, and source-culture very appealing to the continent's sons and daughters in the Diaspora.

Think of the magnetic charisma of Kwame Nkrumah and how many Diasporic Africans made their first pilgrimage to Ghana largely or partly because of him—the Ghanaian trajectory of W. E. B Du Bois can hardly be discussed outside of the politics, appeal, and charisma of Kwame Nkrumah. Think of the beehive of Black Diaspora activism that was the Conakry of Sekou Toure. Stokely Carmichael and Harry Belafonte stoked the fires of Black cultural and musical internationalism with Mariam Makeba and Hugh Masekela when they were all in Conakry. Think of Léopold Sédar Senghor, Mwalimu Julius Nyerere, Nnamdi Azikiwe, Patrice Lumumba, and so many others in their league whose leadership and praxis of heroism made Africa such an appealing proposition to her children in the Diaspora in the twentieth century.

This model of African heroism, I believe, found its culmination in the praxis and brand that was Madiba Nelson Mandela. This global icon made return narratives very compelling and irresistible for the Black Diasporic self. Ladies and gentlemen, please don't tell me that you do not know that Oprah Winfrey's emergency discovery of her Zulu ancestry back in 2006 had a great deal to do with the Mandela magic and appeal. Ms. Winfrey was not alone. We need not run through the list of African American celebrities who discovered their South African ancestry because of Nelson Mandela.

If you look at things closely, the discovery of African ancestry tended to move to wherever the star of a great, transcendental African nationalist hero and statesman was shining. All roads of ancestry discovery once led to Accra before the fall of Kwame Nkrumah; then the roads made a detour and led to Conakry before Sekou Toure became what he became; then the roads migrated to South Africa because of Madiba. If, tomorrow, Nigeria gets her act together and produces a towering global leader of impeccable ethical stock, I wager that many Diasporans will discover their Yoruba, Igbo, or Hausa-Fulani ancestry.

Act One, Scene Five

The passing of Madiba Nelson Mandela to a glorious African ancestorhood has a special significance for our purposes here today. Mandela's death effectively signals the end of the era of the modes of personal, transcendental nationalist heroism and statesmanship which his generation had held out to Africa and the Black Diasporic world. His exit effectively closes the era of those who gave Africa and the Black world such affirmative praxes as "African Personality," "Black Pride," cultural nationalism, and political nationalism. These were the people who were so instrumental in providing the justification for the Caribbean self to seek psychic and cultural anchorage in a matricial idea of twentieth-century African heroism. When Countee Cullen and twentieth-century Black Diasporans asked, "What is Africa to me?," Africa's nationalists and statesmen and women provided answers in their words and actions, especially during the era of the anti-colonial struggle. You saw Kwame Nkrumah and Julius Nyerere, and you had a pretty good idea of what Africa was to you.

But Mandela's death also came on the cusp of a very significant moment for Africa and the rest of the world. Mandela made his exit at a time when what has been described as "the selfie generation" was taking over the commanding heights of global culture through the formidable power of social media. Charles Blow (2014) of the *New York Times* has appropriately defined the selfie generation as folks between the ages of eighteen and thirty-three. In other words, the selfie generation comprises young people. I am assuming that the members of the Caribbean and African Association of the University of British Columbia who invited me here to deliver this lecture today are all generation selfie. Ladies and gentlemen, is this true? Ok, Mr. Blow asserts, also correctly, that one defining characteristic of the selfie generation is that you are the first generation that has not had to adapt to the internet, to social media and allied technologies. In essence, you are citizens of the internet by birth. You are the original owners of what I suggest we call "appsland."

If you are tempted to think that Mr. Blow is stretching things a bit by saying that members of the selfie generation are the only authentic natives of the internet who have not had to adapt to anything, just think of what happens to you when you are not a member of that generation and you try to do things like them without first learning the rules of engagement. Let's say your name is Barack Obama. You go and take a selfie with the beautiful prime minister of a European country, and you get into a load of trouble.

But taking selfies is not all they do in the selfie generation. Members of the generation are driving global culture and agendas in significant new ways. They are asking questions and raising issues. With them, the revolution is televised live in your living room. You saw them in Tunisia, Egypt, and the rest of the Arab world. You saw them in Turkey and Brazil. You saw them all over the streets of America in the Occupy Movement. You saw them live in Ukraine during the Orange Revolution and more recently. I live in Ottawa. I see them carrying placards in front of Parliament all the time. I saw them in my own country in Occupy Nigeria. One foolish aide of the Nigerian president who has tragically fallen into the wrong column of history even described them as "the collective children of anger." All over the world, the selfie generation is the new cool.

I think it is unfortunate that the rise of this generation coincides with the collapse of that particular mode of heroism that is tied to the praxis of genuine nationalists and statesmen and women in Africa. What is Africa to me? For the Caribbean self in the twentieth century, that question was answered significantly by the quality of leadership that the continent had to offer especially in the context of political nationalism and the struggle for freedom. If the selfie generation in the Caribbean and elsewhere in the Black Diaspora asked the same question today—what is Africa to me?—what sort of answer would they get? Just what is Africa offering them?

This is a question that has detained me since I delivered the keynote lecture at the International Leadership Platform Conference of the University of Johannesburg and the Africa Institute of South Africa a few weeks ago. Among the many issues raised by the brilliant and generous discussant of my lecture, Professor Peter Vale of the University of Johannesburg, was the question of leadership and role modelship for the youth of Africa after the demise of the continent's nationalist and statesmen-and-women generation, symbolized by the passing of Mandela. "Where are the leaders and role models that Africa is offering these young people?" Professor Vale had queried. We kept citing dead African statesmen and women . . .

As a teacher in the classrooms of North America, I encounter variations on this question all the time from Nigerian students of the selfie generation. These are undergraduate kids born in Canada or the United States. They've never been home. When they pronounce their Yoruba or Igbo or Ijaw or Edo names, those names end up looking like mangled victims of a terrorist attack. They are Nigerian kids of the new Diaspora. And they stop you after class and ask: "Professor, tell me, why should I have a stake in Nigeria? Why should I visit Nigeria? What's in Nigeria for me?" There are selfie generation kids from the fifty-three other countries in Africa torturing their professors in Canada and the United States with such questions. There are African American and Caribbean kids of the selfie generation asking these questions. Whether they are Africa kids of the old or new Black Diaspora, the selfie generation is not asking—what is Africa to me?—for that is so old school, so Countee Cullen and his generation. Rather, these kids are now asking: What's in Africa for me?

In essence, the selfie generation of the old and the new African Diaspora asks questions that cannot be answered easily. The nationalist, the statesman, the orator, the charismatic leader, the philosopher king—all that ended with Nelson Mandela. Today, the leadership landscape in Africa is so abysmal that you dare not tell the selfie generation to look up to the current crop of heads of state and heads of government across Africa as credible role models and heroes. To the Caribbean and Black Diaspora self, Africa is currently offering a selfie of abysmal, uninspiring, and disgraceful leadership.

You only need to look at the current leadership of the two major states in Africa—Nigeria and South Africa—to appreciate the full extent of the tragedy. In South Africa, the current president is a certified clown, a huge joke. In Nigeria, aides of the current president [n.b., Goodluck Jonathan (2010–2015). —Ed.] consider an extraordinary achievement the rare moments in which he successfully places one incoherent sentence after another incoherent sentence in scripted or unscripted speeches. He is a dour, uninspiring, and corruption-friendly man.

Elsewhere, the news is not any better. Omar Bashir of Sudan and Uhuru Kenyatta of Kenya are customers of the International Court of Justice; Faure Gnassingbe of Togo and Ali Bongo Ondimba of Gabon are scions of presidents for life who may continue that continental tradition; Yayi Boni of Benin and Alassane Ouattara of Cote-d'Ivoire are offspring of the financial philosophy of Bretton Woods. And we have not even mentioned the Paul Biyas, the Teodoro Obiangs, and the Blaise Compaores of Africa. There is just no leadership worthy of our attention at the moment in Africa. Among the current crop of African heads of state, I'm afraid there are no transcendental statesmen and role models worthy of recommendation to the youth of Africa and the Black Diaspora as worthy role models. Luckily, there are stateswomen in the ranks, but their inspirational stories are the rare exception and not the rule.

In essence, in the absence of the Mandelas, Nkrumahs, Senghors, and Nyereres of this world, the selfie generation in Africa and the Black Diaspora is the first generation to stand in real danger of having to accept Justin Bieber, Kim Kardashian, and even George Zimmerman as heroes as Africa fails to offer them credible heroes and genuine role models in the public sphere. The selfie generation is growing up in a celebrity culture powered by American TV. Yesterday, as I prepared to fly here from Ottawa, George Zimmerman was on CNN signing autographs at a gun show somewhere in America. Occasionally, Africa has the good fortune of being able to ward off the danger posed to the selfie generation of Africa and the Caribbean by the globalized reckless celebrity culture of America. Africa tells those kids: don't look at George Zimmerman, look at Lupita Nyong'o. But, like the female presidents, these luminous examples don't come in nearly enough numbers.

What's in Africa for me? Perhaps the search for an answer is what has led Africans of the new Diaspora in the selfie generation (born in Europe and North America post-1980s) to Afropolitanism, the new cultural fad on the block. This is not the place for me to go into the debate on Afropolitanism. Google it. Beyond Achille Mbembe's philosophic-discursive take on Afropolitanism, pay attention to what Taiye Selasie and her followers say it is. Pay attention to why Binyavanga Wainaina says he isn't an Afropolitan. That is your Google assignment.

What is of interest to me here is that Afropolitanism seems to be the last refuge of a new African Diasporan selfie generation in search of ways to log on to a continent that is offering very sparse cultural Wi-Fi access in terms of credible role models in the public sphere. But at least they've got Afropolitanism, those selfies of the new African Diaspora. What about the kids of the old Diaspora in Black America and the Caribbean who cannot describe themselves as Afropolitans and who do not belong in the generation of those going to weep at doors of no return in Cape Coast, Goree, and Badagry? What's in Africa for them?

Perhaps they and their Afropolitan peers ought to look in the direction of the collective cultural heroism of their peers in Africa. Out of nothing, their peers in Africa invented and developed Nollywood into the world's second largest movie industry. Nollywood to a great extent has broken the monopoly of Western modes of representing Africa for the Black Diaspora. And out of Ghana, Africa and the Black Diaspora is swaying to the rhythm of Azonto. Although transcendental nationalism, heroism, and statesmanship of the Mandela type may be dead in Africa, Nollywood and Azonto, with all their warts, are powerful selfies of cultural heroism that Africa is offering the world as a window into the regenerative power of what Kwame Nkrumah once famously referred to as "the African genius." The genius of the selfie generation is also taking over the African street and making very loud statements. I know that the Anza Club is still open in Vancouver. I know that it is still the place where Africa goes to meet the Caribbean on the dance floor twice a week. Perhaps, after listening to this lecture, some of you are going to make your way there this weekend to sway your hips to Azonto. I expect to see your selfies on Instagram!

Face Me, I Book You

Writing Africa's Agency in the Age of the Netizen

I owe the title of this lecture partly to the Nigerian poet, Amatoritsero Ede, who recently "booked" a fellow Nigerian writer for "facing" him in a Facebook spat and, partly, to my favorite palm-wine tapper in Isanlu, my hometown in Nigeria. Although Ede (2011) coined the brilliant expression, "Face Me, I Book You," I think the greater debt is owed to my tapper. I call him my tapper extremely cautiously because he also tapped wine for my father for decades, becoming my tapper only after Dad passed on in 2007.

My palm-wine tapper needs no introduction to an Africanist audience. You know him. He is an eponymous subject, still very much part of whatever is left of the bucolic Africa "of proud warriors in ancestral savannahs" (Diop, 1974), who fired the imagination of David Diop, Léopold Sédar Senghor, and others in the Négritude camp but irritated Wole Soyinka, Es'kia Mpahlele, and other opponents of Négritude's "poupées noires" version of Africa to no end (Damas, 1937). You know him.

You know him because his craft is ageless and has defied the frenzied and chaotic wind of postmodernity blowing over Africa. "Baba Elemu"—that's what we

---

Keynote lecture delivered at the African Literature Association, Dallas, April 2012. Sponsored by the Graduate Students' Caucus of the ALA.

call a palm-wine tapper in Yoruba—is still alive and kicking in towns and villages all over West Africa. Firoze Manji of Pambazuka once busted my West African monopolist bubble by telling me that they also know the palm-wine tapper in East Africa. You know him.

You know him because the fruit of his labor episodically irrigates your tongue whenever summer research takes you to those parts of Africa where he still plies his trade. His black and rusty Raleigh bicycle, the ageless gourds and tired plastic containers attached to the rear end of the bicycle (carrier in Nigeria)—all bubbling and foaming at the mouth—and the dark brown belt of reeds that has gathered mileage by taking his ilk up and down the trunk of palm trees since Obatala got drunk in the mythic process of creation, are all icons of a certain version of Africa that will just not go away. You know him.

In addition to this generic portrait, my own palm-wine tapper is always a vital source of reconnection with my roots during summer vacations in my hometown. Connoisseurs of the matter at hand know only too well that nothing beats the early morning harvest, especially if it comes undiluted with water. That is why the palm-wine tapper has to beat even the most auroral farmer to the belly of the bush. The palm tree knows how to reward the tapper who sets forth at dawn.

Whenever I'm back home to spend some time in Nigeria, the pact between my palm-wine tapper and me ensures that he wakes me up around 6:00 a.m. on his way back from the bush with my own reserved portion of "the usual." I suspect that one of his kegs was named for me or I was named for it as Achebe was named for Victoria, queen of England. He fills it faithfully every morning and his "akowe, mo ti gbe de o" (Book man, I've brought your wine) is my muezzin's call to prayer.

I did not hear my tapper's call to prayer on this particular day in the summer of 2008. The jarring clang of TuFace Idibia's "African Queen"—I'm sure you all know that song—was what woke me up. One of my nieces in the village had been kind enough to set the said song as my ringtone. "You are my African queen, / the girl of my dreams. / You take me where I've never been." That was Idibia crooning in my cell phone. Who could be calling that early in the morning? I concluded that it must be some friend back in Canada or the US who'd forgotten the time difference between Nigeria and North America. I hissed and fumbled for my phone in the grayish darkness of the early morning, and the voice that came from the other end made me jump up in bed.

"Akowe!"

"Akowe!"

That was my palm-wine tapper phoning me—wait for this—from the bush! As I later found out when he returned from that morning's sortie, he was calling me from the neck of one of his trees. He wanted to let me know that delivery would be delayed that morning and I may not get my regular quantity of "the usual." Funny things had happened to his gourds. I understood. In the village, strange spirits disguised as villagers sometimes climbed trees to help themselves to the fruit of another man's labor. It was all part of the territory. I told him not to worry. I would accept whatever he was able to supply.

Then it hit me like a thunderbolt! The familiar and the strange. The uncanny. Try to imagine an elderly palm-wine tapper atop a palm tree in the village, reaching for his pocket to bring out his BlackBerry in order to discuss the laws of supply and demand with a customer whose father he had also served decades earlier under a totally different economy of meanings, and you will understand why that event, in the summer of 2008, marked a turning point in my attempts to fashion new ways of listening to so many new things Africa seems to be saying about her historical quest for agency—a quest that has lasted the better part of the last five centuries.

I also began to think seriously about how the new economies of agency emanating from Africa pose serious challenges to the work of the imagination in the postmodern age of social media and immediate communication. In thinking along these lines, I haven't been too far away from the epistemological challenges which confronted another thinker, another place, another time. I am talking of Walter Benjamin's (1939/1969) attempt to grapple with the rise of the image—film and photography—and its impact on the work of art in his famous essay, "The Work of Art in the Age of Mechanical Reproduction."

The Age of Mechanical Reproduction? That's so dinosaur now! Perhaps you will agree with me that until a BlackBerry joined the arsenal of tools and implements that my palm-wine tapper took atop his trees every morning in Isanlu, he belonged in a habitus of tradition governed by those mytho-ritualisms of existence which has led to tensions in the arena of historical discourses and counter-discourses about Africa's agency. My palm-wine tapper *sans* his BlackBerry comes from the world we have come to associate with Chinua Achebe's *Things Fall Apart*—especially the world as the people of Umuofia knew it before Obierika's famous metaphor of the rope and the knife—or Birago Diop's "Breaths"—where we must "listen to things more often than beings" in order to hear the voice of fire, water, wind, and bush.

This is the world of cosmic equilibrium to which the poet persona in Abioseh Nicol's poem, "The Meaning of Africa" (n.d.) returns after ironically escaping the world of the cold northern sun which gave my palm-wine tapper his BlackBerry. You will recall that after loving the sophistication of Dakar, Accra, Cotonou, Lagos, Bathurst, Bissau, Freetown, and Libreville, Abioseh Nicol's poet persona was advised to "Go up-country, so they said."

The poet-persona is advised that the real Africa of his ancestors is up country in the bush. The story of agency as it relates historically to Africa is easy to narrate from this point. Europe encountered this Africa of "mute ancestral spirits" and "hidden hearts," called her horrible, Conradianly dark names, and proceeded to deny her agency through a series of historical violations and epistemic violence, which bear no rehashing here. As disparate and contested as they have been, Africa's and her Diaspora's epistemological responses to these violations have been fundamentally about the recovery of agency.

We named these responses Négritude, Pan-Africanism, cultural nationalism, decolonization, just to mention a few. In the process of articulating these robust responses, Wole Soyinka and Es'kia Mpahlele may have gone after Senghor; Ali Mazrui and the Bolekaja troika may have gone after Wole Soyinka who, in turn, went after some of them as neo-Tarzanists; Mongo Beti may have gone after Camara Laye for publication of work not sufficiently anti-colonialist; and Obi Wali may have gone after English-language dead-enders, opening the door for Ngugi wa Thiong'o's decades-long crusade against Europhonists. I don't think that anybody would quarrel with my submission that these tensions and disagreements are more or less what the Yoruba would call the multiple roads leading to the same market. That market is the recovery of the self, recovery of agency.

In the stretch of essays and books from "Dimensions of African Discourse" (1992) to *The African Imagination* (2001) and, lately, *The Négritude Moment* (2011), Abiola Irele has done remarkable work mapping the evolution of and the tensions inherent in Africa's counter-discourses of self-recovery. Writing from a different philosophical perspective in the essay, "African Modes of Self Writing," Achille Mbembe (2002) takes a somewhat dismissive tack absent from Irele's work but nonetheless identifies three historical events—slavery, colonization, apartheid—as fundamental to the two currents of discourses and processes of self-recovery that he identifies as central to the question of agency: Afro-radicalism and nativism.

What is interesting for me—and I believe for numerous readers, critics, and followers of Mbembe—are the weaknesses he ascribes to both traditions of discourse in his attempts to problematize them. To Afro-radicalism, he ascribes a "baggage of instrumentalism and political opportunism," and to nativism, he ascribes a "burden of the metaphysics of difference." I wonder what my brother Adeleke Adeeko thinks of that particular critique of nativism, but I digress.

My reading of Mbembe's essay has shifted over the years from a fundamental disagreement with his characterization and insufficient contextualization of Afro-radicalism and nativism to what I am beginning to think are gaps and silences in his critique of the African imagination. These gaps and silences pertain to the very nature of Africa's agency even within the ideological politics and the economies of self-recovery in the African text. For we must ask: what sort of agency does Africa really acquire in Négritude and cultural nationalism? I am talking about the version of Africa which Chinua Achebe, Senghor, Birago Diop, Mongo Beti, Ferdinand Oyono, and Abioseh Nicol rescued from Europe's post-Enlightenment philosophers and colonialist writers. Which agency does Africa acquire in the texts of these *shons of the shoil?*

Which agency does my palm-wine tapper acquire as he moved from Conrad to Achebe? I think his transition is a move from being silent and unspeaking in one textual world to being rescued but spoken for in another textual world. One world gives him to us in body parts, capable only of dialects or incomprehensive babble, tapping a horrible alcoholic brew consumed by lazy natives in irrational quantities, an activity he gets to perform only if he escapes poisonous snakes, lions, and hyenas. Another textual approach restores the cosmic harmony of his world, the ancestral dignity of his work, and treats his product, palm wine, as worthy of the elevated cultural registers and aesthetic apprehension that Africa's violators would normally reserve for merlot, cabernet sauvignon, or pinot noir.

The flora, fauna, and seasons of his world, especially the palm tree, also become subjects of elevated aesthetic treatment. If, as Adam Gopnik, the Canadian essayist for *The New Yorker,* assures us in his Massey lectures, the Romantic imagination elevated winter and ice to art and aesthetics, Achebe and his contemporaries would do much more for the world of the palm-wine tapper in their attempt to fully restore his agency. Don't forget that harmattan and even the white froth and foam of palm wine became worthy elements of metaphorical constructions.

But the tapper is still spoken for in and by these texts. In at least one instance, he is upbraided for killing trees in his youthful exuberance. I am thinking here of a different version of the problematic that Linda Alcoff evinces in her well-known essay, "The Problem of Speaking for Others." Race and gender are weighty dimensions in Alcoff's treatise on the pitfalls of speaking for the native, the oppressed, or the gendered subject. What happens if Africa is the subject that is spoken for or represented, albeit in the ideological resistance mode of Afro-radicalism and nativism, by the privileged African intellectual, especially the writer?

African feminism's critique of Négritude's treatment of African woman and African womanhood provides part of the answer. We must all remember that Mariama Ba and her contemporaries, writers and critics alike, got tired of Négritude's constant conflation of Mother Africa and the mothers of Africa. Yet, in the beautiful and memorable lines such as "Négresse, ma chaude rumeur de l'Afrique" and "Femme noire, femme nue," the Négritude poet actually believed that he was conferring agency on his subject.

In his earlier cited essay, Mbembe approaches this part of the agency question in a manner which allows me to offer possible windows into the dilemmas of representing Africa's agency by writers in my generation. "Over the past two centuries," writes Mbembe, "intellectual currents have emerged whose goal has been to confer authority on certain symbolic elements integrated into the African collective imaginary."

I think my problem as an intellectual arose that morning in Isanlu when a momentary cognitive scission occurred and denied me the ability to "confer authority" on the intrusion of a symbolic element such as a BlackBerry into the imaginary of palm wine as I used to know it. It was immediately obvious to me that what was happening was beyond what could be explained by the usual recourse to the tradition-modernity binary, with the attendant intimations of how Africa negotiates modernity by gradually appropriating, domesticating, or integrating it within her own orders of experience.

From the top of his palm tree, my palm-wine tapper was articulating his own agency and self-representing in ways that are miles ahead of the imaginaries which underwrite my work as a writer and critic. That, I posit, is the problem of African art in the current age of social media and MAC, my acronym for mutually assured communication. The fact that he phoned me from the top of a tree in the bush rattled and unsettled me. What if, God forbid, my Baba Elemu had also recorded videos of himself at work and posted it on YouTube as these new possibilities of agency now afford him? What if he tweets his conversation with me from the top of that tree? What if he makes a photo of himself at work the cover of a Facebook page dedicated to tapping? What if . . . questions, questions, questions.

In a way, I think the writers of Négritude and cultural nationalism escaped these dilemmas not because they shared coevality—or restored it where it was denied—with the palm-wine tapper but because they operated as artists in the age of mechanical reproduction which, as revolutionary as it was, still allowed the possibility of a certain "inert" version of Africa that could be "rescued," "re-represented," and "spoken for" in their texts. My second submission is that this inert version of Africa, on behalf of whom Afro-radical and nativist discourses and praxes were articulated, now speaks for itself in ways that perpetually confound art and the imagination. Coping with an Africa which no longer needs your powers of metaphorical mediation to articulate novel forms of agency, which have the added power of immediate global circulation, is one of the most formidable dilemmas facing the generation of African writers, artists, and intellectuals to which I belong.

Chris Dunton and I have edited some special issues of journals in which we described these new writers, in the case of Nigeria, as the third generation. That description of convenience has been vigorously challenged. My good friend Abdourahman Ali Waberi, also a keynote speaker in this conference, has famously described that generation of writers as "les enfants de la postcolonie" in the case of our Francophone counterparts. Jacques Chevrier at some point was moving the idea of "migritude writers," but I haven't followed the critical fortunes of that concept. Thanks mostly to the Nigerian members of this generation who have been winning bucket loads of international literary prizes—I am almost blushing with nationalistic pride here—the work produced by the children of the postcolony is now globally known and is the subject of numerous panels in conferences such as the ALA.

I am thinking of Helon Habila, E. C. Osondu, and my maternal cousin, Segun Afolabi, who have all won the Caine Prize. There is Chimamanda Adichie and, also, Tricia Adaobi Nwaubani, who did well in the Commonwealth competitions. There is Teju Cole, who recently won the Hemingway Prize here in the US. Oprah made the fame of Uwem Akpan, and a hefty manuscript check confirmed Helen Oyeyemi's arrival on the global literary scene. To these we must add other bright representations of new African writing, especially the novel, such as Binyavanga Wainaina, Monica Arac de Nyeko, Petina Gappah, Leonora Miano, Alain Mabanckou, Abdourahman Waberi, Dinaw Mengestu, Hisham Matar, and Ellen Banda-Aaku, my cowinner of the Penguin Prize for African Writing.

So, we have a cast of writers and a new writing that now whets critical appetites at international conferences. My concern is whether we are paying sufficient attention to the extraordinary dilemmas that these writers face in their attempts to write a continent which now possesses the ability to self-write, self-inscribe, and self-globalize even before the first sentences of their novels, poems, and short stories take shape in their heads. How do you write a continent which no longer lies inert to be rescued from misrepresentation? I saw hundreds of responses and counter-discourses from the African street to the "Kony 2012" video before Teju Cole and Mahmoud Mamdani offered their famous responses. In Twitter and Facebook years, the writer and the scholar were light-years behind the African street. To bring this dilemma back to my point of departure, how should this generation write my BlackBerry-wielding, self-inscribing palm-wine tapper? Reduce palm wine and BlackBerries to conflicting metaphors and inscribe that conflict in flowery prose? That would be too simplistic.

Besides, there is a second problem. Those who wrote Africa's agency in the age of mechanical reproduction never really had to deal with new forms of art that competed with and challenged the ontology of their respective mediums of expression. The novel, the short story, the poem, the play, and the painting didn't have to worry too much about other forms of generic expression emerging at once as evidence of Africa's new ability to self-represent and also as contending and competing forms of art. This lack of competition, if you ask me, partly accounts for why the scribal form of the African imagination, enjoyed an imperializing prestige over oral forms much to the consternation of colleagues like Karin Barber and Thomas Hale.

Tricia Nwaubani's (2009) excellent novel, *I Do Not Come to You by Chance,* sadly, does not enjoy the luxury of not worrying about competition for its ontology as a form of art which seeks to represent a particular reality of post-SAP Nigeria in terms of its local and international dimensions. What do you do if you are writing a novel about what, for want of a better description, we must call Nigeria's 419 letters (Ferguson, 2012) and the imaginaries that have now come to be associated with them, only to discover that those letters themselves are now being discoursed and critiqued as art forms on their own terms? Where the 419 letter now stakes a vigorous claim to an ontological identity as art, does a novel which ventures into its territory even merit the description of simulacrum? Which art is representing what? It is almost now possible to claim that the 419 letter waiting in your mailbox as you listen to my lecture here is art representing the reality that is Nwaubani's novel. If your head is not spinning yet, please remember that some actors in Africanist scholarship here in North America have been very active in making a case for 419 emails as an art form worthy of critical reflection. I have received at least one solicitation in the past to help evaluate submissions to a planned special issue of a scholarly journal on 419 letters as a literary genre.

As I speak, the same argument is being made for the literary quality and generic integrity of tweets. In Canada, where I am based, the literary establishment seems to have made up its mind that the tweet is a literary work. Now, that's tricky because it makes every tweeter a potential writer just as a collection of somebody's Facebook status updates or 419 letters could give us a Nobel Prize for Literature down the road. If you look at the website of Canada Writes where the CBC organizes the prestigious CBC Literary Prizes, you'll be able to assess the considerable energy devoted to tweets and tweet challenges. A tweet is literature as far as Canada Writes is concerned.

The Nigerian writer, fiery critic, columnist, and cultural commentator, Ikhide Ikheloa, has been screaming himself hoarse about the need for African writing to face these new realities. Like Obi Wali, decades ago, Mr. Ikheloa has been making very weighty pronouncements on the future of African writing. And he is arguing, among many pro-social media arguments, that tweets, Facebook updates, and the associated genres of the social media age, would leave African writers behind if we don't come up with imaginative ways to engage the forms of continental agency which they throw up. The way he sees it, social media is a significant part of the future of African writing and he has been warning that writers in my generation, especially those who remain social media stone agers, are in danger of extinction.

I take Mr. Ikhide's work extremely seriously and follow him religiously online. You should google him, follow him on Twitter, and add his blog to your daily reading. When he is not upbraiding African writers in the new generation for not taking the full measure of the possibilities of the social media revolution for our work, he is making very valid points in terms of the contributions of social media to even our own agency as writers.

Let me explain my understanding of Ikhide's position. Errors of interpretation would be mine. I think the debate about which audience the African writer ultimately writes for is further complicated for my generation by the mediators who stand between our work and our audiences. A measure of that is how much of Africa we still literally translate or italicize in the actual process of writing. Go to any Nigerian novel and see what happens with registers and diction depicting the actualities of youth experience, counterculture, and postmodern cityness for instance.

Paraga, mugu, maga, yahoozee, aristo, shepe, etc., all capture experiences which the Nigerian writer in my generation italicizes to mark their strangeness and otherness. Yet, Western writers using other Englishes in Britain, Canada, New

Zealand, Australia, and the United States don't always feel compelled to capture local experiences in italics. Just last month, Elizabeth Renzetti (2012), a Canadian columnist writing for the *Globe and Mail,* had this to say about the extensive registers of drunkenness in England:

> The English have more words for drunk than the Inuit have for snow, perhaps because it is as much part of the landscape. On a given night, you might be bladdered, legless, paralytic or rotten with drink . . . I thought I'd heard them all until British Home Secretary Theresa May used the phrase "preloaded" on Friday to announce her government's war on binge drinking. Preloading refers to the act of getting hammered before you go out to get hammered—that is stocking up on cheap booze from the grocery store in order to be good and wobbly by the time you hit the bars.

"Bladdered," "legless," "preloaded"—all registers of English drunkenness. Would a British writer in my generation italicize these experiences specific to his own people in a creative work? You guess is as good as mine. "Stop Italicizing Africa!" Ikhide screams at writers in my generation all the time on Facebook. "Stop writing Africa for your literary agents, publishers, editors, marketers, and Western liberals," Ikhide screams. Perhaps Ikhide already suspects that there is a reason why Salman Rushdie and Paulo Coelho—more international writers are following their example—have quietly migrated a great deal of their art, celebrity, and mystique to Facebook. "If your handlers insist on an italicized Africa, take your agency to social media and engage the world freely," Ikhide screams at African writers.

I hope I am not the only one who takes Ikhide extremely seriously.

What Does (Nigerian)
Literature Secure?

When I first received the theme of this conference in a somber email from the dean of the Faculty of Arts, University of Ibadan, I wondered what writerly demons took possession of my dear friends Professor Remi Raji, Richard Ali, Denja Abdulahi, D. M. Dzukogi, and other members of the National Executive Council of the Association of Nigerian Authors, and made them settle on a theme advertising such apparently incompatible terms as "literature" and "security" in the same sentence. Being a very active member of literary Cyberia (my neologistic contraction of Cyber and Nigeria), I could understand and relate to the social media part of the theme but security? National security? Was it the demons of audacity? Was it the demons of limitless and unbounded imagination, a sine qua non of our trade as writers?

Being traffickers in what Vaclav Havel, our Czech literary kindred spirit, calls "the art of the impossible," I guess it is not too difficult to imagine a group of Nigerian writers, gathered somewhere (perhaps at Abe Igi in the National Theatre), struggling to hear each other above the thunderclap of Boko Haram's bombs, the

Keynote lecture at the National Convention of the Association of Nigerian Authors in Uyo, Akwa Ibom State, Nigeria, November 9, 2012 threnodic rat-a-tat of armed robbers' machine guns, the riotous skid of kidnappers' getaway vehicles, the boom of petrol tankers exploding daily on our roads, or passenger buses suddenly thinking themselves cruise ships and taking a plunge in the river, especially in a country where setting forth at dawn is no longer an act of self-preserving prescience, our roads, skies, waterways, and half-existent railways being permanently famished; no, it is not too difficult to imagine that writers thus assaulted by the choric banality of mass deaths in this nation-space would exclaim at some point: What can we do? What is our role in all this? What can literature secure? Does literature secure?

But the assault on the senses is not merely auditory. It is also visual for our Republic of Noise—the noise of death—also offers a generous daily quota of crimson contemplation, of morbid ugliness to the eye of the citizen-beholder. Increasingly, our ways of seeing (apologies to John Berger) are clouded by the unavoidable contortions of human forms whose body fat feeds the flames consuming them, victims of the latest madness of necklacing mobs. The victims come younger and younger. You take your eyes off the raging inferno fed by the body fat of a mad country's youth only to confront a spectacle common in the land, radically different from what Léopold Sédar Senghor of Négritude fame had in mind when he penned one of the most memorable poetic paeans to the naked body of the black woman in these lines: "naked woman, black woman / clothed with your colour which is life / with your form which is beauty!"

No, the naked body on visual offer in our Nigerian case is not the stuff of poetic jouissance and Négritude aestheticization. It is the body of the latest victim of the mob. It is the eponymous body of the pubescent or post-pubescent Nigerian female, stripped naked on campus, at the bus stop, in a mall or in any other imaginable space of quotidian errands; stripped naked by her male compatriots for stealing a BlackBerry, an iPad, or even a recharge card. In essence, were it even remotely possible for our putative "Abe Igi" group of writers to escape the auditory evidence of national insecurity all around them, they must still contend with the interpellative authority of the visual, especially in the age of social media, where violence and the desecration of the human effectively belong in the economy of viral dissemination made possible by YouTube, Facebook, and Twitter. Sooner or later, these assembled writers must confront the question: What can we do? What is our role in all this madness? Can literature help?

If I am mapping a possible route taken by ANA EXCO to theme and sub-themes that shall exercise us in this convention, "Literature and Security," it is because I am mindful of a certain Aristotelian dilemma in framing the very purpose of

Nigerian literature. It is true, this dilemma has always been with us insofar as project nationhood has been one bloody trajectory from colonial dehumanization to the deadlier afterlives of colonialism, but the Kafkaesque nature of our postcolonial present makes it all the more urgent for us to interrogate it. And the dilemma is this: if one of the key thematic strands of Aristotle's theory of Art, especially in *Poetics,* is the much bandied about notion that art imitates life, I believe we have reached that moment in our national unraveling when writers can legitimately begin to exclaim: Art we see and know but, pray, where is life? Where death in its physical, spiritual, and metaphorical actuations dragoons a nation into what Frantz Fanon (1952/2008) famously calls "the zone of nonbeing," and life is marked more by its absence—or its painful emptiness when present—how does art fulfill that Aristotelian imperative of imitating life?

Although he comes into this argument from the standpoint of his philosophical engagements with religious fundamentalism, one of the postcolonial discontents emptying Nigeria of life, of too many lives too quickly, followers of Wole Soyinka's various attempts at a Cartesian engagement with the national specter of insecurity and death would agree that his discursive move has a double entendre. In other words, Soyinka's various appropriations of the Cartesian cogito in his public intellection—"I am right, therefore you are dead" "I am dead, therefore I exist"—serve as pointers to the intractable nature of this particular form of national death and prefigure the perplexity of the artist. The said perplexity brings the artist to a fundamental question: in a nihilistic national context, where death increasingly boasts its own ubiquitous ontology, when is art? Alternatively, as I am framing it here, what does or what can literature secure?

These dilemmas about literature, art, and security would be a nonstarter if Africa, and Nigeria in particular, had been able to reach a Platonic nirvana which is said to be the desire of states and political entities. You may not remember many things about Aristotle, but I am sure you recall that, in certain ways, he was a rebellious student who bothered little with gerontocracy. To put it in Nigerian parlance, Aristotle nor get respect for elders. This explains why they said Aristotle would exercise his intellect developing a workable theory of art imitating life while his great, illustrious teacher, Plato, preferred the easier option of banishing art and the artist from his own ideal Republic. Indeed, were Plato a Nigerian, he would by now have been rewarded with a GCON, keeping the illustrious company of Aliko Dangote and Mike Adenuga, for evincing a situation in which the state wouldn't have to worry about art and artists.

In essence, the proper place to begin to problematize the intermesh between literature and security is the physical and corporeal integrity of the artist, the writer in our case. After all, a Yoruba adage says that when a man proposes to adorn you with rich new clothes, perhaps the most expensive lace material in town, it is proper to pause and examine what he himself is wearing. In the build-up to this conference, the moment word got out that I would be your keynote speaker, I received a number of interview requests from journalists on the ground here in Nigeria. Alas, I was only able to grant one. One of the questions that I was asked pertains to the journalist's conceptualization of the theme of this conference. "How can writers help in solving the socio-political, economic, and security problems that Nigeria is mired in," the literary journalist, Awaal Gaata, asked me. This question evokes the proverb I only just deployed about a stranger's promise of new clothing. When writers in a nation under siege are forced to confront the incubus of insecurity from the standpoint of a possible Aesculapian role for their art in society, we must pause to ask whether literature has ever secured the writer himself.

Of the three national solitudes evoked in the interview question above—i.e., the role of literature in socio-political, economic, and security problems—I believe we can pass quickly, even if somewhat superficially, on number two—economic problems. Even if you are a Chika Unigwe, and you published a fantastic novel, *On Black Sisters Street,* which has just earned you ten million naira in prize money, there is only so much you can do to contribute meaningfully to solving Nigeria's economic woes as a writer. In fact, if I may throw in some yabbis into this discourse, speaking of writers and economics or economic security, I must confess that I nearly changed my mind about answering the call of the Muses when I got to Ibadan in the early 1990s and saw Odia Ofeimun's beaten and battered seventeenth-century Volkswagen Beetle!

The second solitude, literature and socio-political issues, has a longer and stronger purchase tied to the modes of emergence and the ideological contexts of modern African literatures, related as they are to the epochal high points of what Okwui Enwezor has aptly called Africa's "short century." The charged, recovery-of-the-self atmosphere of the twentieth century, which nurtured such ideological signposts as Pan-Africanism, Négritude, cultural nationalism, and decolonization, and produced radical discourses of African/Black agency typified by Frantz Fanon, Amilcar Cabral, Walter Rodney, and our own Chinweizu, produced a deontology which linked our literature to socio-political issues. What Achille Mbembe famously calls African modes of self-writing connects our literatures, especially Nigerian literature, with the praxis of political and cultural agency in very significant ways.

In other words, ours was mainly a literature of protest and commitment to struggles framed on the socio-political front. Art, we said, was not for art's sake in Africa. You need not go farther than the literary-essayistic careers of Chinua Achebe and Ngugi wa Thiong'o in the last four decades for affirmation of this point. Similarly, the art and essayistic interventions of Nigeria's radical generation of writers in the 1970s and 1980s also point to this vision of art as socio-political praxis. I am thinking here of Odia Ofeimun, Niyi Osundare, Femi Osofisan, Bode Sowande, Olu Obafemi, Tunde Fatunde, Abubakar Gimba, Wale Okediran, and Festus Iyayi, among others.

The third solitude, literature and security, is the most slippery. I have proposed that we start that excursus by examining the writer's own clothes. Tying the idea of literature and security to the corporeal integrity of the Nigerian writer is not an epistemic move I am proposing just because the realities of the age of transnational terrorism, defined by what the radical leftist thinker, Tariq Ali (2003), has called "the clash of fundamentalisms," have forced nation-states such as America to shift the meaning of national security from its neoclassical roots in the survival of the state to the survival and personal security of the individual citizen. This is no egg-and-chick conundrum. The modern nation state understands that the personal security of the citizen precedes and gives birth to national security. The formation of an American Department of Homeland Security, with its focus more on securing the life of citizens in the American homeland, is emblematic of this shift toward the personal in contemporary understandings of national security.

More than this shift, however, I am proposing this move because the personal security of the writer in a nation-space that does not just see the writer as a threat to its Platonic utopia but has also completely demissioned from its sacred mandate of guaranteeing the security of the individual is a subject which cuts painfully close to the bone for Nigerian writers. The discontents of nationhood and the self-inflicted madnesses of the Nigerian project have cost us the precious lives of three writers, including a former national president of this esteemed association. We lost Christopher Okigbo. Then we lost Mamman Jiya Vatsa—I remember him every time Richard Ali posts something about ANA's Abuja plot of land in the Facebook publicity desk he runs for ANA. Then we lost Ken Saro-Wiwa.

No, poetry did not save these three writers. Literature did not secure them. It did not secure Wole Soyinka either. The only consolation art offered Soyinka, as it has done for every writer jailed for his or her art or activism, is to be an *exutoire,* an outlet. Africa's prison narratives, from Soyinka's to Jack Mapanje's and Ngugi's, bear testimony to this paltry consolation. The recent kidnapping of Hope Eghagha, one of our notable poets and novelists, is Nigerian insecurity's way of reminding our literary family that even if she is no longer killing or jailing us, she is still infinitely capable of terrorizing us by whizzing the cap off our creative heads.

However, which artist has art really saved and secured in this direct sense? When has literature literally stood between the writer and the gallows? We can count the examples on the tip of our fingers. The abundance, sadly, lies in those who have perished for art's sake. The abundance lies in writers who have been endangered, imperiled, hounded, silenced, or simply rendered irrelevant for art's sake. Odia Ofeimun's (1998) opening paragraph in his essay, "Postmodernism and the Impossible Death of the African Author" is instructive:

> In 1968, [writes Ofeimun,] the year Roland Barthes, the French philosopher announced the "Death of the Author," Wole Soyinka was in detention for opposing the prosecutors of the Nigerian civil war. The poet, Christopher Okigbo, had been killed in the early skirmishes of the war. Chinua Achebe was in exile, engaged in matters as distant from the literary as raising funds for and campaigning for the rise of the Biafran Sun. Mongo Beti was in Paris on a contested visa, his book soon due for banning in both his Camerounian homeland and France. Naguib Mahfouz's book, *Children of Gebelawi*, was banned in his country. Camara Laye was on the run from Sékou Touré's gendarmes. Can Themba had drunk himself to death in a Joburg shebeen. Bloke Modisane, overwhelmed by the depression of exile, was reported to have jumped down from a New York skyscrapper, Alex La Guma was still incarcerated on Robben Island. And Dennis Brutus, freed from Robben Island, was in exile as was Ezekiel Mpahlele and many other South African writers. One case parodied the other. The fortunes of the producers of African literature was evidently in such dire straits that it would not have required a stretch of the imagination to grasp what the French philosopher was talking about.

The point must be made that just as Soyinka (1981) took on French poststructuralist critique and a certain strand of Nigerian literary criticism it engendered in his essay, "Barthes, Leftocracy, and other Mythologies," Ofeimun in his own essay is confronting the hegemon of postmodernist theorizing and its attempts to deconstruct the writer into extinction. In the mad rush to detotalize and atomize master narratives by a Europe that had fallen into intellectual ennui after two disastrous wars, the author in postmodernist canard became a location, a text that had exhausted its own possibilities of regeneration. Ofeimun is trying to show that the latest European theoretical fad has little or no meaning for African literature. However, by painting such a graphically gory tableau, the author of *The Poet Lied* inadvertently raises the question of literature and security in the African context.

With Ofeimun's essay, my questions return with all their deliberative force: Whither art in the security of the artist? What guarantees the corporeal integrity of the writer? Does literature secure? If so, what does literature, Nigerian literature, secure? When, faced with Nigeria's quotidian threats to life, the Christian sings, "only Jesus can save, only Jesus can save, alleluia," and the Muslim responds with a similar affirmation of the Holy Prophet's ability to save him; what is the writer's recourse? Does he declare himself the "god of poetry" and crawl with Uzor Maxim Uzoatu into "the shadow of pagan poverty," hoping that the violence and insecurity across this land shall consider him too poor and economically unviable for elimination? Does he acknowledge the obvious fact that art is not law enforcement and does not save in a literal sense?

Perhaps that last point—art does not save—is not entirely true? Art saved Scheherazade or, more precisely, literature saved her life. That's perhaps the most famous evidence we have of literature's direct intervention in the business of security, the business of preserving life, instead of merely farming metaphors and other figures of speech to imitate or represent it. However, Scheherazade's journey to life via the instrumentality of literature comes with a severe warning to the lazy writer. To live, Scheherazade had to enter the history books as one of the most prodigious—if not the most prodigious—storytellers of all time. She had to spend one thousand and one nights telling one thousand stories at the rate of one story per night. She could not afford boring stories laced with tired metaphors and worn clichés. She had to invest her stories with what André Breton and his fellow French surrealists call the poet's ability to take the familiar and divest it of every trace of its familiarity. Yet she had to sustain this imaginative flow for a thousand and one nights. Excuse me, folks, but that's like asking Toni Kan, the author of the fascinating volume of short stories, *Nights of the Creaking Bed,* to make that creative bed creak every night for one thousand and one nights or else . . .

Closer to us in time and space, art saved life or deferred death during the Zulu wars. Of the many narratives of the Zulu wars, I particularly like one that comes more from the street stories that have crystallized into myths about that war. For instance, in an interview clip in the documentary movie, *Amandla,* Hugh Masekela (2002) reminds us that the Zulu warriors also had their own Scheherazade moments. They would sing so beautifully, so melodiously, that the advancing imperialist armies would temporarily lay down their arms to enjoy the singing. "Wait, wait, let them finish that beautiful song before we kill them," the imperialists would exclaim, "we can't kill them while they sing so beautifully!" Although Professors Toyin Falola and Moses Ochonu, two of Nigeria's brightest gifts to the discipline of history, warned me as I prepared this lecture that the claim of art intervening to save lives or to put death in temporary abeyance belongs more in the province of legend and mythologies that war inevitably generates than in the archives, I kind of like the sound of that myth all the same!

I don't just like the fact the Zulus created a lore in which their soldiers resorted to art, musical aesthetics to be precise, to freeze the enemy like the gaze of the Medusa. I also like the fact that two eminent Nigerian historians reminded me that war creates lore, legend, and mythology. In other words, wars generate narratives. The phases of existential crisis through which a people pass in the historical trajectory toward nationhood also generate accompanying narratives. By mapping these narratives, through time and space, we begin to get a handle on what it is exactly that literature secures beyond the paltry examples of Scheherazade and Zulu warriors turned emergency artists. We begin to get a handle on what Nigerian literature has tried to secure ever since a literary corpus emerged, branded by that national identity.

Reflecting on the universal dimension and symbolism of the South African struggle during his recent Steve Biko memorial lecture, our brother Ben Okri provides a useful window into the form of security which literature and the arts guarantee. Okri conceptualizes a people's historical march as an upward progression toward what he calls the mountaintop. The hint of *The Pilgrim's Progress* is unmistakable. So is the hint of the Ayi Kwei Armah of *Two Thousand Seasons.* Not every people is privileged to reach that mountaintop, Okri alleges. In other words, most people crawl and crawl, fording the mythological seven rivers and seven mountains but ultimately still never reaching the mountaintop. This explains why Armah sums up Africa's march to the mountaintop as "a thousand seasons wasted wandering amazed along alien roads, another thousand spent finding paths to the living way" (Kwei Armah, 1972).

For societies lucky enough to reach the mountaintop, or to at least get close enough to catch a glimpse of it, here is what Okri (2012) believes they bequeath to humanity from that auspicious location:

> The value of mountain-tops is not to live on them but to see from them. To see into the magic and difficult distances, to see something of the great journey still ahead;

to see, in short, the seven mountains that are hidden when we climb. It may be only once that a people have such a vision. Maybe very, very great nations have such a vision a few times, and each time they do they affect a profound renewal in their history and take a quantum leap in their development. Most nations never glimpse the mountain-top at all; never sense the vastness and the greatness of the gritty glory that lies ahead of them in the seven mountains each concealed behind the other. Maybe Ancient Greece saw such a vision a few times and dreamed up its notion of a flawed democracy and left its lasting legacy in its architecture, its literature, but above all in its political structure for unleashing its genius upon the world. Maybe Ancient Rome saw such a vision a few times too and built straight roads through history, wresting with the idea of freedom and tyranny and conquered a sizeable portion of the known world, and left for us their ambiguous legacy of empire, literature and might.

Witness the recurrence of literature in Okri's account of the legacies which ancient Greece and ancient Rome have bequeathed humanity from the mountaintop. This recurrence, I must add, is not due to professional bias on Okri's part. The author of *The Famished Road* is merely foregrounding one of the fundamental functions of literature. That function inheres in the terrible power of fictional truth to secure memories of not just the past but of a future foretold, and inscribe such narrativizations in trans-temporal dimensions, which come to determine how future generations encounter and engage a people's march toward the mountaintop. In essence, a people's march toward the mountaintop is also a function of the stories they tell to temporalize their epic struggles. Not every society reaches the mountaintop, warns Okri, and that is true. Methinks, however, that every society tells and records the story of the march, of triumphs and travails, of failures and successes, of reversals and progress, of ups and downs, of heroism and betrayal, of war and peace, of love and hate.

Fictional truth secures these memories and acquires an authority superior to other modes of recording. This trans-temporal authority of fictional truth is the only reason why we view ancient Greece today largely through her arts, mostly her literature and architecture. Think of the trials and tribulations of that society during the years of the Peloponnesian War. Think of *The History of the Peloponnesian War*, a magisterial account of that war written by the great historian, Thucydides, and ask yourselves why our civilization, looking back at ancient Greece today, prefers memories of that war and era secured by the fictional truths of the Greek tragedians, especially Sophocles and Euripides. Why does our current civilization prefer to gaze at ancient Rome through the fictional truths of a Virgil than the documentary accounts of a historian like Tacitus?

The answer to these questions is bad news for my earlier-mentioned professional historian friends, Professors Toyin Falola and Moses Ochonu. For, I am saying that a thousand, two thousand years from now, a future civilization will look beyond the archives constituted by disciplinary history and privilege the truths secured by Nigerian fiction today as a window into how we negotiated our march toward the mountaintop, the roads taken and the road not taken (apologies to Robert Frost), how we lived, laughed, loved, and hated. How we kidnapped. How we bombed. How we killed. How we pogromed. If, as it is tempting to predict, given our talent for self-inflicted national injuries, we somehow never make it to the mountaintop, we need not worry. Our literature will secure that failure against forgetting.

Why do people privilege the security offered against forgetting by literature and the arts? Does it have something to do with the aphorism that when the chips fall wherever they may, literature and the arts are the only evidence, the only trace that a civilization truly leaves behind? Civilizations whose skeletal remains defy even radiocarbon dating have left us the marvel of rock paintings. When the artist Victor Ekpuk looks for what remains of his forbears, the only window he has left to reconnect with them is the scribal art that has defied time, Nsibidi. Does the privileging of the security offered by literature and the arts have something to do with man's fundamental instinct of self-preservation? Does a civilization disappear, confident that evidence of its passage through time has been secured by the scribal talents of her writers and artists?

I got a near answer to these provocations sometime last year on a Nigerian listserv. More on internet listservs later, but suffice it to say that listservs are part of the internet revolution which has extended the boundaries of the imagined in the imagined community that is project Nigerian nationhood. There are alternative imaginaries of nationhood going on in listservs, especially among Nigerians in the Diaspora. Thus it was that somebody posted one of those grating, provocative commentaries of Wole Soyinka. We know that Soyinka's essayistic interventions in Nigeriana do not fail to provoke passionate reactions.

That particular intervention of his considerably irked a respected Nigerian professor of mathematics in Canada. The professor in question boasts a mouth-watering CV in his field. I cannot emphasize it enough that he is one of our very best. Yet, in a remarkable display of intellectual collapse, he rushed to the listservs lambasting Soyinka. Soyinka needs to be humble, says our professor of mathematics. Those who win the Nobel Prize in Literature should understand that theirs is inferior to the Nobel Prizes in the sciences. Where laureates in mathematics, physics, chemistry, and medicine are talking, Soyinka should be humble and keep quiet or he should hold a rapid dialogue with his legs. I am not making any of this up. It's in the archives of Nigerian listservs. The mathematician was not done yet. What exactly is it that literature even contributes to society? Only the sciences, the hard sciences, have any bearing on human development, he enthused. Literature, writers, only tell stories to entertain us, and we humor them by listening to them. Folks, imagine what would have happened if this professor, who doesn't think that literature offers much beyond storytelling and entertainment (he subsequently tried hard to do damage control while essentially not giving up his claims), had heard that the Association of Nigerian Authors had dared to gather to reflect on the role of literature in security! He would have had a heart attack.

On my own account, after miraculously escaping a cardiac arrest from reading the professor's reflections vis-à-vis the worthlessness of literature and the inferiority of the Nobel Prize for Literature compared to its illustrious elder brothers in physics, mathematics, chemistry, and medicine, I wanted to intervene in that thread. I was still contemplating where or how to begin when Oluwatoyin Adepoju, a ubiquitous literary presence on Nigerian listservs, recovered from his own shock and exclaimed, among his several responses to the subject matter, that literature and culture are the windows into how peoples across times have domesticated and applied science. He averred further that the security of the sciences depends on how they are imagined and narrativized by the civilizations they inhabit and such narrativizations are often the world's and history's window into a particular culture. I saved my breath after Mr. Adepoju's intervention. He had said it all. I didn't need to jump into the thread by pointing out Gyan Prakash's (1999) work, *Another Reason: Science and the Imagination of Modern India,* on the role of science in colonial India and how imperial narratives of the native ultimately defined how science was applied to his body and environment in line with the overall objectives of empire. Even almighty science is subject to narratives—a.k.a., the art—of its own becoming.

Writers are the world's window into a culture. That was a key aspect of Mr. Adepoju's contribution to the discussion in question. In essence, those looking back at today's Nigeria a thousand years from now will detect evidence of our literature's attempts to offer the security of a predicted future. They will read Wole Soyinka's *A Dance of the Forests,* Chinua Achebe's *A Man of the People,* and the Menippean satires of T. M. Aluko, especially *Chief the Honourable Minister,* and glean evidence of the errors of the rendering. They will gain insights into how fictional truth imperils the artist ironically through its own vatic function. Let's not forget the reaction to *A Dance of the Forests* by a political establishment which, like the dog, failed to hear the hunter's whistle and perished in the forest of postcolonial anomie.

If it is clear from the foregoing that beyond Scheherazade, beyond Zulu warriors turned musical aesthetes, Nigerian literature offers the security of memory and the armor with which to shatter the carapace of forgetting; it is equally pertinent to add that the vatic essence of fictional truth is an attribute which makes it a very dangerous truth indeed. Although societies across time and civilizations have preferred to disdain the forms of mnemonic security a writer has to offer through his art, casting the writer as a Cassandra figure, often never believed until writerly prescience has become regrettable actuality down the road, the truth is that society has a fatal attraction to, a love-hate relationship with the writer's truth. This truth places a double-edged sword in the hands of the writer. Tell the truth and be damned; don't tell the truth and be damned.

In the attempt to secure memory and social history with this double-edged sword, the writer often discovers that the security, which his work guarantees for the social body, is hardly ever coterminous with the security of the writer. There is often a terrible opportunity cost: secure memory and forego your own security. This is true because society hardly accords the writer the privilege of value-free, personal remembering. Neither does the writer enjoy the privilege of exercising other forms of prose that are not deemed to carry the authority of fiction. Those of you who have read Salman Rushdie's new memoir, *Joseph Anton,* would have followed that writer's rude introduction to this double jeopardy. If he wrote fiction and entitled it *The Satanic Verses,* trouble! If he wrote nonfiction and entitled it *Imaginary Homelands,* wahala!

Chinua Achebe is, of course, currently caught up in these tensions between a writer's prose, a writer's security, and the security of public memory. I do not wish to rehash the arguments for and against Achebe, but we are all aware of the current situation with *There Was a Country* (2012). We may raise legitimate questions about the memory the book secures: Is it the memory of Biafra? Is it the memory of Nigeria? Is it both memories in their overlapping, fractal, and fratricidal actuations? For my purposes here, that is not where the issue lies. The point, for me, is to try to understand why a writer's act of remembering—among the mountains of scribal acts of remembering on all sides of our civil war tragedy—is the most susceptible to generating national hysteria. And of all the reactions to Achebe's book, I am interested in knowing what seems to have conferred an extra authority on an act of counter-remembrance by another writer. I am talking of Odia Ofeimun's extended treatise, "The Forgotten Documents of the Nigerian Civil War."

I raise this point because Northrop Frye, perhaps the twentieth century's most significant critic of literature and prose, has a few things to say about memoirs and autobiography. According to Frye (2006),

> autobiography is another form which merges with the novel by a series of insensible gradations. Most autobiographies are inspired by a creative, and therefore fictional, impulse to select those events and experiences in the writer's life that go to build up an integrated pattern. This pattern may be something larger than himself with which he has come to identify himself or simply the coherence of his character and attitudes.

Frye goes on to trace the mutations of this intensely personal form of prose to the confessional modes of St. Augustine and Jean-Jacques Rousseau.

If what Frye, and indeed, most theorists of creative nonfiction—the genre which houses memoir and autobiography—have to say above is true, it raises the question: why is Achebe not allowed to recollect or select aspects of his life in tranquility? And why are reactions to Ofeimun's counter-remembering just as passionate, just as heated? The answer is simple. The nonfiction prose of both writers enjoys the symbolic authority of their fiction. There is such a thing as a symbolic capital that comes with the designation "writer," which makes ordinary things suddenly become extraordinary when touched by a writer. History and its scripting become extraordinary the moment two writers, Achebe and Ofeimun, enter into its domain, hence the passion.

If there is a generation of Nigerian writers whose relationship to project nationhood carries the burden of these tensions between social memory, public memory, and security, it is, undoubtedly, my generation. I don't know why this is so, but we sometimes use our friend, Harry Garuba, as the borderline between the generation of the seventies and the early eighties and my own generation. For critical convenience, the critic Chris Dunton and I have edited peer-reviewed international journals in which we called mine the third generation of Nigerian writing, a designation that has not come without controversy. Obu Udeozo prefers the expression, "third wave writing." The publication of Harry Garuba's *Voices from the Fringe* in 1988 effectively marked the coming out parade of this generation. Most of them are poets. We were still more than a decade away from the rise to dominance of prose fiction beginning from the 2000s, a rise enhanced no doubt by an avalanche of international literary prizes by members of my generation. But in the late 1980s to the early 1990s, Nigeria's social memory expressed itself mainly in the poetry of my generation.

If you examine the social memory inscribed in the poetics of my generation from the perspective of what it sought to secure it from—or against as the case may be—you will discover that the idea of which nation's memory is being secured becomes quite fuzzy, quite uncertain, shorn of a unifying center, such as ritual or mythopoeia, which had tied the works of earlier generations to project nationhood. No matter how expansive and how ambitiously itinerant the imagination is, it is always possible to detect a silhouette of either the national or the ethno-national center in the poetics of Achebe, Soyinka, and Clark; in the restless social realism of Osundare, Osofisan, Obafemi, Okediran (what a succession of Os!), and Iyayi, whose novel, *Violence,* typifies this trend. To the question—was there a country?—the work and praxis of the generations before mine had an answer: yes, Nigeria.

With the poetry of Obu Udeozo, Uche Nduka, Idzzia Ahmad, Remi Raji, Obu Udeozor, Ogaga Ifowodo, Olu Oguibe, Afam Akeh, Chiedu Ezeanah, Obi Nwakanma, Amatoritsero Ede, Nduka Otiono, David Diai, Obi Iwuanyanwu, Nnorom Azuonye, Toyin Adewale, Nike Adesuyi, Angela Nwosu, and Unoma Azuah, the answer to that question becomes as tentative as it is contested. Harry Garuba has astutely used the poetry of Emman Shehu as an inroad to the loss of the unifying ethno-national center in Nigerian literature with the advent of my generation. Therefore, even if this poetry speaks to the socio-political problems of the world it inhabits, which Remi Raji tries to gather into bowls of laughter in *A Harvest of Laughters*—I suspect it is the bitter laughter that his people call "erin oyinbo"—we get the constant hint from this generation that a transnational imaginary is the only security against the atrophy of project nationhood.

Perhaps it has something to do with the fact that this generation of writers is the literary contemporary of Andrew, that eponymous popular-cultural character who first offered flight as a praxilic response to generalized insecurity. So, Remi Raji, Olu Oguibe, Ogaga Ifowodo, Obu Udeozo, and so many others, went on to invest in an aesthetics of that-which-is-home-but-not-recognizable. While the body of the poet was willing to remain rooted as we see in Oguibe's canonical poem, "I am Bound to This Land by Blood," the spirit must free itself and roam to mine security and succor in a transnational world that is precariously claimed, as we see in Afam Akeh's poems thematizing England, Uche Nduka's "Aquacade in Amsterdam," Amatoritsero Ede's "Globe Trotter," and the direction that Remi Raji's creative sensibilities took in the collection, *Shuttle Songs America,* and a recent travelogue published on Facebook, dedicated to his Ukrainian poetic peregrination.

Speaking of Raji "publishing" creative nonfiction on Facebook, the rise of Cyberia poses the question of border security in a very real, literal sense. The phase of Nigerian writing which houses writers I don't even ever have to meet face-to-face to feel like I've known them my whole life, largely because they have social media personas, is an interesting phase indeed. It is an age where literature has been nervous about losing the book form as we know it—I first heard about this anxiety from Nadine Gordimer way back in 2000 at a conference I attended with Harry Garuba in Pretoria. It's a long way now from the year 2000, and those intervening years have seen Nigerian literature gradually migrate to Cyberia, first as listserv discourse with the birth of Krazitivity in 1999, to the rise of Nnorom Azuonye's Sentinel literary empire with its poetry bar, and now to the efflorescence of forms of literature associated with blogs, Facebook, and Twitter.

Richard Ali, Tolu Ogunlesi, A. Igoni Barrett, Ifedigbo Nze Sylva, Jumoke Verissimo, Chinyere Obi-Obasi, Egbosa Imasuen, Uche Peter Umez, Ukamaka Olisakwe, Paul T. Liam, Su'eddie Vershima Agema, Onyekachi Peter Onuoha, Rosemary Ede, Saddiq M. Dzukogi, and so many brilliant writer-citizens of Cyberia, face border security problems beyond the simple threat to the book. There is a democracy that comes with social media, and it has radically transformed the idea of the writer. Everybody with a BlackBerry and a blog is now a potential writer. We may wax puritanical here, declaring that we know who a writer is; the problem is with cultural shifts in the West that seem to validate the idea of a nomenclatural borderlessness when it comes to who is a writer in the age of social media. For instance, in Canada where I reside, Canada Writes organizes tweet challenges in which they ask writers and aspiring writers all over the country to condense creative writing into tweets. But the pressure for the writer to become a netizen increases by the day. Salman Rushdie and Paulo Coelho are social media celebrities. In our case, I sometimes fear that the fiery US-based literary and cultural critic, Ikhide Ikheloa, may soon require a certificate of social media occupancy to consider a Nigerian writer worthy of his attention.

It is in this expanded context, where literature is increasingly determined by very loose understandings and definitions, that our emergent crop of writers must try to secure not just the social memory of their own generation. This new cultural context challenges their very ability to own stories devolving from our national experiences, good and bad, in the global marketplace of creativity. What does it mean, for instance, that one of the most powerful accounts of South Africa's attempt to exorcise the ghosts of Apartheid through the truth and reconciliation framework has been written by an American? I am sure you have heard of the blockbuster novel, *Absolution,* by Patrick Flanery? What does it mean that the novel that will probably settle the argument over the national origin of 419 is not Tricia Adaobi Nwaubani's *I Do Not Come to You by Chance* but a novel recently published by a Canadian writer, which has just been awarded Canada's biggest literary prize, the Giller Prize? The ownership of stories South African and Nigerian by an American and a Canadian writer has been facilitated largely by social media. We live in days and times when a Tibetan monk can write an authentic Nigerian story, in an authentic Nigerian voice, after spending a year on Twitter and Facebook.

A generation owned the idea of a homeland and narrativized it in terms of unifying rituals of self-recovery from rape that was colonial. When the morning after set in shortly after independence and disillusionment weighed heavy on the soul, another generation of Marxist and quasi-Marxist hotheads tried to press social realism into the service of a struggle against self-inflicted postcolonial injuries in the 1970s and the 1980s. A subsequent generation, mine, tried to secure forms of attachment to that homeland despite the inevitable pull of the transnational moment. Now, a new generation must deal—or is it cope?—with the existence of a parallel world which admits of no boundaries whatsoever, be it geographical or even the old boundaries that secured the identity of literature, differentiating creative prose from other forms of writing. It is also a world in which ownership of national imaginaries is no longer easy to determine as a piece of flash fiction could appear anywhere as a Facebook update, telling stories we thought we owned. When social media expands democratic access to the Other's story and changes the dynamics of its ownership, what Nigerian stories will our vibrant new generation of netizen-writers own? On whose terms are they going to tell those stories? Mark Zuckerberg's?

I thank you for your time and patience.

Post-centenary Nigeria

New Literatures, New Leaders, New Nation

I guess it's the water. Something must be in the water that members of Nigeria's literary fraternity and sorority drink which makes them see a direct connection between prosperity Pentecostalism—as we experience it in Nigeria today—and their own calling in the Republic of Letters. I do not need to tell anybody in this room that Pentecostalism of the prosperity ilk owns the copyright to the narrative and actuality of miracles in the lives of the citizens of this country. Indeed, so gripping is the national preoccupation with miracles and portions as the immediate dividend of democracy, sorry, of faith, that our Muslim brethren are determined not to be left out of the scramble of each Nigerian to claim his portion and possess his possession. A video recently went viral on social media of a Muslim cleric in full public performance of the stage rituals of a prosperity Pentecostal pastor delivering miracles of healing and material reward. Miracle workers are the new cool, and I am starting to have a nagging suspicion that folks believe that literature, like prosperity Pentecostalism, is a miracle worker.

Two years ago, my good friend, Professor Remi Raji, national president of the

Keynote speech presented on November 13 at the 2014 MBA International Literary Colloquium in Minna, Niger State

Association of Nigerian Authors (ANA), and his energetic team in the ANA National EXCO, invited me to deliver the keynote lecture at the ANA National Convention in Uyo, Akwa Ibom State. The topic they asked me to address is what created my initial suspicion that Nigerian writers may inadvertently have come to subscribe to the notion that literature, like the prosperity Pentecostal pastor, has become a miracle worker. I was asked to explore the role of literature in national security. And I asked myself: save in the province of miracles, how is literature supposed to take over the functions of Alhaji Sambo Dasuki and provide us with a national security shield against Boko Haram, kidnappings, armed robbery, and other familiar specters of bloody insecurity in Nigeria?

My suspicion that Nigerian writers believe in the ability of literature to deliver Holy Ghost fire miracles has been confirmed by Baba Dzukogi and all the organizers of this feast of literature and creativity at whose behest we have assembled here today. My brief here is as challenging, as perplexing, as the assignment that Professor Remi Raji and his crew gave me in Uyo two years ago. Today, I am asked to address the theme of newness. As if this wasn't challenging enough as a theme, I've been saddled with the baggage of newness raised to the power of three: new literatures, new leaders, and a new nation in post-centenary Nigeria. In essence, I am asked to examine the possible ways in which our new literatures—however defined and imagined—impact on leadership and nationhood. Let's just hope that the organizers of the Garden City Literary Festival will not ask me to come one day and address the linkages between literature and the provision of good roads, hospitals, and sundry infrastructure!

Now, the adjective, *new,* has been used to qualify three nouns in our topic, but we can only confidently bear witness to the truthfulness of one as far as Nigeria is concerned. New literatures? That is true, very much true in this country. New leaders? That's a lie, for we do not even have old leaders let alone new ones. New nation? That also is a lie, for we are more remarkable for our violations of every definition of nationhood than for a will to the emergence of a nation, new or old. These, of course, are contentious considerations that we shall return to in due course. Suffice it to say, for now, that I do not want you to take my apparent dig at the theme of the Uyo conference and our theme here today too seriously. It's a lighthearted way of approaching the crux of my brief. It is just banter; my way of getting back at those who have saddled me with the onerous task of showing the ways in which literature is indeed the only human institution capable of imagining miracles and delivering on them. This pregiven essence of literature isn't always obvious. Only the seriously lettered can understand that no human advancement—civilization, the Enlightenment, modernity, science and technology—happened outside of storying and narrativizing.

In essence, I am saying that those who in Uyo dreamed of the ability of literature to open up and probe new imaginaries of national security and those who in Minna have asked me to interrogate the ability of our new literatures to map new narratives of nationhood and leadership are writers who understand that the word and the story have been at the foundation of every human enterprise from the beginning of time. If we are inclined to go back as far as ancient Greece and Rome, we will remind ourselves that the content, shape, nature, character, and identity of those two political expressions of civilization and human organization took their inchoate foundational steps in the narratives of the storyteller. Ancient Greece and Rome were not just imaginaries that became political realities, they were imagined and narrativized in epics, myths, legends, and even dramaturgy of the tragic ilk. Subscription to the interpellative power of these narratives is what confers on them legitimacy and hegemony. They acquire an amniotic essence of national histories and identity. The national epic is the most powerful source of identity for the modern nation and the nation-state.

Think of what Homer's *Iliad* means for ancient Greece. Think of what Virgil's *Aeneid* means for ancient Rome. Think of *The Tale of Genji* for Japan; of *La Chanson de Roland* for France; of the *Epic of Gilgamesh* for Iraq; of *Ramayana* for India; *Beowulf* to Anglo-Saxons and Britain. Think of all these national epics and you come to an understanding of the fact that literature indeed has the miraculous power to forge the essence and the spirit of a nation—and of a nation-state depending on the level of legitimacy and hegemony it acquires across time. From Ernest Renan to Benedict Anderson, no scholar of nation, nation-state, and nationalism has ever made short shrift of the centrality of the creative imagination, of stories, of myths and legends to the emergence and enabling of the lineage of nation and nation-state.

That is why Benedict Anderson defined nation as an imagined community. "Literature is Fire" screams the Peruvian Nobel laureate, Mario Vargas Llosa, in a 1967 lecture he delivered on being awarded the Romulo Gallegos Literary Prize in Venezuela. Vargas Llosa agrees on the centrality of literature to the soul of nation and nation-state in the said essay. Literature is fire! If literature is fire, what does this mean for those of us who are writers and workers in the field of creativity and imagination? It reminds us that literature is Promethean. You will recall that the first time man is said to have stolen from the Gods—I would have called it man's first act of corruption but, luckily for us, stealing is not corruption in this country—what he stole was fire! Prometheus stole fire from the gods and gave man the miracle of creation and creativity. Literature is fire! Literature is miracle. Literature makes miracles!

Long before ANA National thought of the prophylactic powers of literary imagination, long before the conveners of this edition of the MBA International Literary Colloquium thought of a theme which connects literature to imaginaries of leadership and nationhood, generations of writers before us have imagined the connections between literature and project nationhood. It could not have been otherwise. At the political level, Nigeria may have been a product of colonial will, violence, and desire. She may have been an economic contraption cobbled together by Lord Lugard and named by Flora Shaw for the benefit of Great Britain. Nigeria's first generation of writers in the English language—the producers of what we now conventionally call modern African literatures—were not going to allow the original injury of our foundation—colonial dehumanization—to become the basis of postcolonial project nationhood.

Two factors aided the task of this generation in terms of imagining a postcolonial becoming for Nigeria. First is the fact that they were coming from an oral tradition in which art was indissociable from politics. The verbal arts, all our oral genres, served a utilitarian function in traditional society. Thus, the transition to a modern aesthetic of protest and resistance was not such a huge leap for our foundational writers in English. Second, is the fact that these writers came of age in the climate of twentieth-century grand narratives of freedom. This was the age of Négritude, of Pan-Africanism, of the African nationalist struggle, of decolonization. This was the age of the radical liberator, which gave us such figures as Frantz Fanon, Walter Rodney, Amilcar Cabral, Eduardo Mondlane, Patrice Lumumba, Agostinho Neto. This was the age of the grand dreams and ambitions of Kwame Nkrumah, Julius Nyerere, Nnamdi Azikiwe, and all their contemporaries for the continent. Literature slipped into a predictable role as the cultural wing of this struggle.

Achebe served what I consider to be the most direct notice of his generation's mission to deploy art in the service of society and nation in his essayistic career. You are certainly familiar with the essay, "The Novelist as Teacher" (1975). You will recall his clear and oft-reiterated point in many of his essays that the writer cannot be expected to be excused from the task of nation-building and other socio-political debts to his society. More than any transcendental commonality of themes, motifs, and textual strategies in their creative enterprise, I believe that this sense of a socio-political mission, of the need to press art into the service of new imaginaries of nationhood in which a culturally empowered and psychologically decolonized citizenry shall embrace the possibilities of postcolonial nationhood is what came to give these writers the first sense of a generational identity in the annals of Nigerian writing.

Wole Soyinka, for instance, often alludes to a "foundational quartet" of Nigerian letters comprising himself, Chinua Achebe, J. P. Clark, and Christopher Okigbo. We must bear it in mind that the imagination of this foundational quartet was present at the birthing of Nigeria's postcolonial moment. Their creative contribution to emergence of a new nation in those heady years came in the shape of visions and intimations of the roads to be taken, of roads to avoid, of pitfalls that could lead to anomie and errors of the rendering. Indeed, Soyinka (1963) heralded the birth of his new nation with a prophetic play, *A Dance of the Forests.* Achebe (1966) predicted corruption and coups in *A Man of the People.* Okigbo (1964) foretold wars and rumbles of war in *Limits.* By the time we arrive at J. P. Clark's (1981) lamentations of inertia, corruption, and the myriad dysfunctions of Nigerian statehood in his poetry collection, *State of the Union,* it was clear that Nigeria had made Cassandra of this generation of writers at prohibitive national costs.

Perhaps this is why Soyinka looked at his generation in the arts and beyond and famously or infamously described her as a wasted generation? He is not alone. The next set of writers to gain a loose collective consciousness as a generation also had a grandiose ambition and belief in the ability of literature to imagine and will into being a Nigerian nation that would work for a Nigerian people. These writers shook off post-independence disillusionment and disappointment to embark on a radical journey to regain personal and national selves. They had no patience with the eclectic theoretical and aesthetic sensibilities of the Soyinkas and the Achebes of this world. Theirs was going to be hotheaded and fire-spitting Marxism or Marx-influenced discursive and aesthetic radicalism. Think of Zaynab Alkali, Tanure Ojaide, Femi Osofisan, Bode Sowande, Niyi Osundare, Festus Iyayi, Tunde Fatunde, Kole Omotoso, Odia Ofeimun, Wale Okediran, Olu Obafemi, Ken Saro-Wiwa, Abubakar Gimba, Chidi Amuta, Stanley Macebuh, Chinweizu, Biodun Jeyifo, and how they fired up the Nigerian literary scene in the 1970s and 1980s.

Sometime in the early 1990s, Femi Osofisan delivered a lecture at the University of Leeds which contained the report card of his generation in Nigeria—and elsewhere in Africa—as far as their lofty dreams of literature and nation, literature and society, were concerned. Soyinka spoke of a wasted generation, right? Well, Femi Osofisan's (1996) lecture is entitled "Warriors of a Failed Utopia." A certain Nigeria of a certain dream is, of course, the failed utopia captured in Osofisan's lamentation. By the time Osofisan was delivering his lecture, Nigeria had endured the military dictatorships of Buhari/Idiagbon, Ibrahim Babangida, and Sani Abacha. SAP had drained the soul of the Nigerian people and emptied the content of Nigerian nationhood. Corruption was eating up the crumbs left by SAP. The embrace of Marxism and poverty no longer appealed to this generation. Many moved abroad. Those who did not move abroad went in pursuit of capitalism and prosperity.

Wasted generation. Warriors of a failed utopia. Two writers, two generations, two successive grim report cards on Nigeria's stubborn resistance to the Aesculapian functions of literature. My generation should have taken a hint. We should have remembered the tale of the wise tortoise. The tortoise arrived at the entrance of the lion's cave, noticed that all the paw prints of the animals who had gone to pay a condolence visit to the sick king of the jungle were going inside and none was coming out, and took a life-saving hint. The tortoise did not enter the cave. My generation did. We entered the cave of national envisioning because that is what literature commands. I mentioned Mario Vargas Llosa's essay earlier. The crux of his submission in that essay comes down to this statement: "nobody who is satisfied can write." That is Vargas Llosa's (1997) one-sentence definition of the creative vocation. Literature is a permanent dissatisfaction with one's condition, one's environment, one's society, one's community. It is out of the cauldron of that dissatisfaction that literature dares to imagine differently. Art imagines out of a deontology of dissatisfaction. Ask John Lennon.

My generation entered that cave because we were dissatisfied. Just as Soyinka and his foundational quartet were dissatisfied. Just as Femi Osofisan and his warriors of a failed utopia were dissatisfied. To my knowledge, no member of my generation has ever announced our report card the way Soyinka and Osofisan made definitive pronouncements on their respective generations. It could be because our story, our entanglements or lack thereof with project nationhood, is still unfolding. If we won't make that call, if we won't make that pronouncement, there are new kids on Nigeria's literary block. They have been rocking the Nigerian, African, and global literary worlds. These new kids on the block—more on them later—would make the call for my generation. They are that irreverent because they are good at what they do. They would announce the report card of generation in terms of literary accomplishment and in terms of what we did or did not do with the task of literature and nation.

The novelist and poet, Richard Ali, is a one of the new kids on the block. I love Richard Ali. Not in a way that will guarantee me a fourteen-year prison term in Kirikiri. Richard Ali is what you would call my protégé. That is the sense in which I love him. But I am not afraid to say this: God soda Richard Ali's mouth! It was on Richard Ali's Facebook wall that I first chanced upon a thread in which his generation was passing judgement on mine! Their judgement was harsh and unforgiving. Whereas Soyinka and Osofisan had described two generations of wasted or failed warriors in search of a failed Nigerian utopia, Richard Ali and his fellow coroners did a post-mortem on my generation and simply placed a question mark to indicate absence and emptiness where we had been or ought to be. Where are they? What happened to this generation, Richard Ali queried. I dare not tell you the discussion that ensued among members of Richard's generation as they took their koboko and went after us. Trust Deji Toye not to carry last in such a venture.

Nigeria happened to my generation. Incidentally, a poem I wrote about hemorrhage, about Nigeria bleeding us to Euro-America, included in my collection, *The Wayfarer and Other Poems* (2001), was what prompted Richard Ali's reflection on my generation. We did not set out to be exiles. We did not set out to be the Andrew generation whose space is now occupied by Richard Ali's question mark. In 1988, Harry Garuba edited a volume of poetry whose significance remains unsurpassed in the annals of Nigerian letters as far as I am concerned; *Voices from the Fringe* (1988) did for Nigerian letters what Léopold Sédar Senghor's *An Anthology of New Negro and Malagasy Poetry* did for Négritude poetry back in 1948. Senghor's anthology announced the birth of Négritude poetry; Garuba's screamed the arrival of a new generation of Nigerian writers. The critic Chris Dunton and yours truly spent much of the 1990s and early 2000s theorizing these new creative effervescence as the handiwork of those we labeled Nigeria's third generation writers.

This generation did not remain long on the fringe. By the early 1990s, they were the only news in Nigerian literature. Today, those of us who move in Euro-American circuitries of knowledge production on African literatures often marvel at the sort of literary history that is always constructed for Nigeria abroad. You'd think that Nigerian literature went to sleep after the Osofisan generation concluded that they were warriors of a failed utopia and roared back to life only in the 2000s when Helon Habila, Chimamanda Adichie, Chris Abani, Helen Oyeyemi, Sefi Atta, Chika Unigwe, E. C. Osondu, Uwem Akpan, Biyi Bandele, and Teju Cole came to global attention. Viewed from the Global North, it is as if the literary effervescence of the late 1980s to the 1990s never happened.

Yet, the foundation of whatever is happening today in Nigerian letters can be traced to the renewal of creative juices and energies by the generation of Remi Raji, Wumi Raji, Sola Osofisan, Uche Nduka, Olu Oguibe, Obi Nwakanma, Okey Ndibe, Obi Iwuanyanwu, Obu Udeozor, Uzor Maxim Uzoatu, Maik Nwosu, Chiedu Ezeanah, Esiaba Irobi, Ogaga Ifowodo, Toyin Adewale, Omowumi Segun, Nike Adesuyi, Lola Shoneyin, Unoma Azuah, Promise Okekwe, Angela Nwosu, Nduka Otiono, Akin Adesokan, Ike Okonta, Nehru Odeh, Ebereonwu, Eddie Ayo Ojo, Carlos Idzia Ahmed, Emman Shehu, Okome Onookome, and Toni Kan. Obviously, you know that this is a ridiculously short list. I cannot possibly mention all the writers who transformed the Lagos-Ibadan axis and the Nsukka axis into the two dominant literary hubs in Africa in those heady days.

The hemorrhage did happen. Afam Akeh, Olu Oguibe, Uche Nduka, Sola Osofisan, Godwin Amatoritsero Ede, Okey Ndibe, Biyi Bandele started the early trickle toward Europe. Drip, drip, drip and a generational exodus toward Euro-America had become the defining feature of the generation by the end of the 1990s. Is it really true that exile and flight are the only legacy of this generation? I think that exile, flight, absence, and Richard Ali's question mark tell less than half the story of this generation. We must remember that the majority of the members of a generation that has come to be defined by flight and departure did not in fact leave Nigeria.

Toni Kan has always been here. Remi Raji, Uzor Maxim Uzoatu, Chiedu Ezeanah, Denja Abdullahi, Emman Shehu, David Diai, Henry Akubuiro, Omowumi Segun, Toyin Adewale, Nike Adesuyi, Chux Ohai, Jude Dibia, Ike Oguine, Dulue Mbachu, and many prominent members of the third generation never left. Lola Shoneyin, Ogaga Ifowodo, Chuma Nwokolo, and Victor Ehikhamenor (many don't know that he authored *Sordid Rituals* [2002], a volume of poetry) are all back. Ebereonwu and Austyn Njoku never left till they left. To the extent that it is possible to speak of a renewal of literary modes imagining a new Nigeria beyond the ruination of military rape, to the extent that it is possible to speak of an aesthetic split with previous generations, one has to credit the third generation with such specters of literary renaissance. My generation produced the first truly new literature which imagined the Nigerian nation in a new way—marking a rupture with the practices and antecedents of previous generations.

Using mainly the poetry of Emman Shehu, Harry Garuba has described the aesthetic departure of the third generation from the practices of preceding generations in terms of a decentering of the mytho-ritualistic bases from which the first two generations imagined project nationhood. Here, nobody is going to make Ogun or any of the weird characters in *A Dance of the Forests* (Soyinka, 1963) the organizing principle of an imagined nationhood. Nobody is going to invoke the matricial or nativist essence of mother Idoto as a pathway to personal and national becoming. Nobody is going to expect a new Nigerian nation to say yes so that her Chi may echo yes in return.

Even in the context of SAP and military despotism, the evacuation of the mytho-ritualistic center as the basis of engaging and imagining project nationhood led to textual adventurism and thematic daring on a scale previously absent from the Nigerian imagination. Nigeria could now be imagined as a postmodern force field of play in which other emotions, other psychologies, other realities beyond the admonitions of history and culture could be summoned to feed the psychic will and desire of the patriotic self for anchorage in a hostile national space. Consider the difference in the use of laughter as a motif in the poetry of Niyi Osundare and Remi Raji. Osundare's laughter is bitter, the sort of ironic laughter which is said to be worse than crying in Yoruba lore. The reality of the homeland that Osundare is engaging calls precisely for such a deployment of laughter. Laughter in Remi Raji's poetry does not serve the purpose of lamentation. It is indicative of the poet's ability to find spaces of love for a scorched and scorching homeland.

But Remi Raji is not alone. Freedom from the mytho-ritualistic imperative is what accounts for one of the most powerful enactments of patriotic attachment to fatherland in Nigerian poetry. Who could have thought that this could happen outside of a cultural-nationalist praxis involving the salute of a mytho-ritualistic source? But Olu Oguibe (2013) pulled it off. "I am bound to this land by blood," announces the poet persona of his great poem of the same title with considerable gusto. And with this anthem-poem—arguably the most famous poem of my generation—he inaugurated what you could call a poetics of love as the predominant ritual of relating to fatherland in Nigerian letters. In previous traditions, love took the indirect route of admonition, reproach, and chastisement for the errors of the rendering; chastisement for the roads not taken. With my generation, a poetics of boundless love was unleashed.

In fact, if you take a look at their collections in the 1990s, there is hardly any that doesn't contain a section of love poems. We know, since Pablo Neruda and Léopold Sédar Senghor, that love poems addressed to named or unnamed women aren't always what they seem to be on the surface. We know that the body of the named woman or unnamed woman is often a double entendre unto which is grafted an idea of the fatherland, Chile in the case of Neruda, Senegal in the case of Senghor. Study the love poems of Ogaga Ifowodo, Remi Raji, Nduka Otiono, Toyin Adewale, Unoma Azuah, and you will see Nigeria the fatherland grinning at you beyond the silhouette of the male or female partner who is the ostensible addressee of each poem. Those who still pay attention to the poetry of the 1990s at all—remember I told you that they have been silenced as a corpus; Lola Shoneyin is remembered today as the author of *Baba Segi* (2010), nobody remembers *So All the Time I was Sitting on an Egg* (2002); most people will tell you the title of Unoma Azuah's novels, few will remember the title of her poetry collection—focus all their critical energies on the naked denunciation of military rule.

There is one more thing that Nigeria did in terms of imagining Nigeria which I believe has come to characterize the textualities and identity politics of the young writers that have been referred to as post-centenary writers by the conveners of this conference. I have obviously taken the liberty to expand the brief of our discussion so that we do not reduce newness to any generation. Every generation had ways of imagining Nigerian newness, of imagining Nigeria newly. My generation screamed that Nigeria can be loved beyond reproach because we are bound to her by blood. But we also screamed that love for her must never imply limiting our creative energies and imagination to chronicling and narrativizing her. We found ways to extend her into the world in a postmodern actuation of the transnational imperative.

Harry Garuba opines that the extension of Nigeria as a self into the self of the global and the transnational begins in the poetry of Emman Shehu. I think a similar claim can be made for Uche Nduka. After the chronicle of the life of my generation that he offered in the cinematic clip strategy of *Chiaroscuro* (1997), it is safe to say that Uche went on to embrace the world, fashioning a poetics unmoored in immediately localizable national anchors. The embrace of the world. The transnational imagination. The Afropolitan persona. If you move beyond what Uche Nduka has been writing and publishing after *Chiaroscuro*—consider his poem, "Aquacade in Amsterdam"; if you move beyond the Toronto peregrinations of the poet persona in Amatoritsero Ede's "Globetrotter," if you move beyond the imaginative transnational crossings of Chris Abani's (2004) Elvis in *Graceland,* if you move beyond Sarah Ladipo Manyika's (2008) attempt to reproduce the London errantry of earlier generations in *In Dependence,* you encounter a new generation that must grapple with the identity politics of Afropolitanism and the attendant contradictions of trying to imagine a new Nigeria in an existential context which daily reminds them that the world is now their playground.

Not so long ago, when I was cutting my poetic teeth and doing the usual runs in the writing confraternities of Ibadan and Lagos, I had to rely on the good offices of the British Council or the Alliance Française to encounter the world infrequently. I had a Nigeria that could be symbolically sealed off and made exclusively amenable to my imagination and that of my contemporaries. This is not possible for Richard Ali, Tolu Ogunlesi, Paul Liam, Olisakwe Ukamaka Evelyn, Abubakar Adam Ibrahim, Okwui Obu, A. Igoni Barrett, Ifedigbo Nze Sylva, Jumoke Verissimo, Chinyere Obi-Obasi, Egbosa Imasuen, Uche Peter Umez, Su'eddie Vershima Agema, Onyekachi Peter Onuoha, Rosemary Ede, Saddiq M. Dzukogi, and so many other members of the new generation now animating and rocking the Nigerian literary scene.

If a hermetic national locale is not available to them, it is not because they must contend with the deracination of some of their contemporaries who have found their way into Nigeria's literary consciousness while being basically of the Global North—Helen Oyeyemi, Tope Folarin, Chibundu Onuzor, etc. It is not because any of them is carried away by the delusions of Teju Cole and Taiye Selasie whose idea of cosmopolitanism is a disavowal of the tags African or Nigerian writer. It is not because they cannot write creative works set in Nigerian realities—Kaine Agary's (2006) *Yellow Yellow,* Richard Ali's (2012) *City of Memories,* Sylva Ifedigbo's (2012) *The Funeral Did Not End,* Isaac Attah Ogezi's (2012) *Under a Darkling Sky.* It is mainly because new modes of transnational alterity prevent exclusive claims to national conversations.

The impossibility of national exclusiveness is played out daily on social media. This is not just the generation of flash fiction and what I have called twitterature elsewhere; they are a generation whose Nigerian literary conversations must engage the "Nigerianness" of Binyavanga Wainaina, Barbara Mhangami, NoViolet Bulawayo, and Christie Watson. Wole Soyinka and company had for raw material a Nigeria that was brutalized by colonialism and handed over to them. Femi Osofisan and company had for raw material a Nigerian in which the lofty dreams of independence had collapsed, and they went in search of utopia wielding fiery Marxism. My generation had for raw material a Nigeria sapped beyond recognition by SAP and military rape, and we tried out a poetics of love on her. Pa Ikhide's children have for raw material a borderless Nigeria whose literary axes are located not just in Ake and Port Harcourt but also in Kenya, Uganda, and other funny places from which we read the tweets and Facebook their Facebook updates.

This new reality gives them an advantage though. Never mind the complexities and fault lines of Nigeria that we love to retail, all preceding generations had a rough national referent that we could call the single story that is Nigeria, for want of a better expression. Today, the story has been atomized and scattered all over the place like broken China in the sun. That is why Chimamanda (2006) writes *Half of a Yellow Sun,* and we encounter subtle counter-stories in *Musdoki* (Maiwada, 2010) and *City of Memories* (Ali, 2012). Those looking at Nigeria and Africa from the outside may still threaten her with the danger of a single story. The new writers imagining her from within do not run such risks. They have at their disposal not a single story or referent but multiple and fragmented stories. The dilemma we face with a generation in possession of multiple narratives of a single nation in the age of social media is this: will their stories become a thousand flowers armed with the inalienable right to bloom under the sun or will their stories be Babel?

I wish you fruitful deliberations in this conference.

Bibliography

Abani, C. (2004). *Graceland.* New York: Farrar, Straus & Giroux.

Able to laugh at their people, not just cry for them. (1998, June 21). *New York Times.* Retrieved from https://www.nytimes.com

Achebe, C. (1958). *Things fall apart.* London: Heinemann.

Achebe, C. (1964). *Arrow of God.* London: Heinemann.

Achebe, C. (1966). *A man of the people.* London: Heinemann.

Achebe, C. (1975). The novelist as teacher. In *Morning yet on creation day: Essays.* Garden City, NY: Anchor.

Achebe, C. (1977). An image of Africa: Racism in Conrad's "Heart of Darkness." In R. Kimbrough (Ed.), *Heart of darkness* (pp. 251–61). London: W. W. Norton.

Achebe, C. (1999). Africa is people. *Massachusetts Review, 40*(3), 313.

Achebe, C. (2012). *There was a country: A personal history of Biafra.* New York: Penguin.

Acholonu, C. (1995). *Motherism: The Afrocentric alternative to Feminism.* Owerri: Afa Publications.

Adesanmi, P. (2001). *The wayfarer and other poems.* Lagos: Oracle.

Adesanmi, P. (2012). The ABC of a Nigerian joke for western audiences. *Writers Thinking Allowed.* Retrieved from https://writersthinkingallowed.wordpress.com/2012/05/12/the-abc-of-a-nigerian-joke-for-western-audiences-by-pius-adesanmi

Adichie, C. N. (2006). *Half of a yellow sun*. New York: Knopf.

Africa rising: A hopeful continent. (2013, March 3). *The Economist*. Retrieved from https://www.economist.com

Agary, K. (2006). *Yellow yellow*. Lagos: Dtalkshop.

Aidoo, A. A. (1985). *Someone talking to sometime*. Harare: College Press.

Ake, C. (1982). *Social Science as imperialism: The theory of political development*. Ibadan: University Press.

Ali, R. (2012). *City of memories*. CreateSpace.

Ali, T. (2003). *The clash of fundamentalisms: Crusades, jihads and modernity*. New York: Verso.

Amatoritsero, E. (2011). Face me; I book you!: The arts and asocial media. *Maple Tree Literary Supplement,* 10. Retrieved from http://mtls.ca/issue10/editorial

Annan, K. (2014). Ebola crisis: UN launches urgent appeal for donations. BBC News. Retrieved from http://www.bbc.com/news

Attah Ogezi, I. (2012). *Under a darkling sky*. Lagos: Hybun Publications International.

Ayinla, K. (1990). *Fuji Ropopo* [LP]. Nigeria: Kollington Records.

Bates, R. H., O'Barr, J. F., & Mudimbe, V. Y. (1993). *Africa and the disciplines: The contributions of research in Africa to the social sciences and humanities*. University of Chicago Press.

Bayart, J. (1993). *The state in Africa: The politics of the belly*. New York: Longman.

Benjamin, W. (1969). The work of art in the age of mechanical reproduction. In H. Arendt (Ed.), & Zohn, H. (Trans.), *Illuminations: Essays and reflections* (pp. 217–252). New York: Schocken. (Original work published in 1939).

Blow, C. (2014, March 7). The self(ie) generation. *New York Times*. Retrieved from https://www.nytimes.com

Brand, D. (2001). *A map to the door of No Return*. Toronto: Random House.

Carey, J. (1993). *The intellectuals and the masses: Pride and prejudice among the literary intelligentsia, 1880–1939*. New York: St. Martin's.

Césaire, A. (2007). *Discourse on colonialism* (J. Pinkham, Trans.). Marlborough, England: Adam Matthew Digital. (Original work published in 1955).

Chabal, P., & Daloz, J. P. (1999). *Africa works: Disorder as political instrument*. Bloomington: Indiana University Press.

Chinweizu. (1975). *The west and the rest of us: White predators, black slavers, and the African elite*. New York: Random House.

Clark, J. P. (1981). *State of the Union*. London: Longman.

Collins, G. (2013, January 17). The point of lance. *New York Times*. Retrieved from http://www.nytimes.com

Combs, S., Jordan, S., Wallace, C., Betha, M., Rogers, D. J., Jr., Scandrick, M., . . . Finch, R. (1996).

Only you [Recorded by 112]. On *112* [CD]. New York: Bad Boy Records.

Cullen, C. (1925). Heritage. In *Color*. Retrieved from https://www.poemhunter.com/poem/heritage

Diop, D. (1974). Africa. *Massachusetts Review,* 15(3), 506.

Edmonds, K., Reid, A., & Simmons, D. (1991). End of the road [Recorded by Boyz II Men]. *Boomerang* [CD]. Atlanta: Motown Records.

Edoro, A. (2014, October 15). Ikhide versus Binyavanga: The Caine Prize convo—cainerversation—continues. *Brittle Paper*. Retrieved from https://brittlepaper.com/2014/10/ikhide-ikheloa-binyavanga-caine-prize-cainerversation

Edwards, B. H. (2003). *The practice of diaspora: Literature, translation, and the rise of black internationalism*. Cambridge, MA: Harvard University Press.

Ehikhamenor, V. (2002). *Sordid rituals*. Lagos: Oracle.

Elam, H. J., Jr. (2007). Gem of the Ocean and the redemptive power of history. In C. Bigsby (Ed.), *The Cambridge companion to August Wilson* (pp. 75–88). Cambridge University Press.

Emecheta, B. (1988). Feminism with a small "f"! In K. Petersen (Ed.), *Criticism and ideology: Second African writer's conference, Stockholm 1988* (pp. 173–181). Uppsala: Scandinanvian Institute of African Studies.

Enwezor, O., Achebe, C., & Museum Villa Stuck. (2001). *The short century: Independence and liberation movements in Africa, 1945–1994*. Munich: Prestel.

Falola, T. (2012). Nationalising Africa, culturalising the West, and reformulating the humanities in Africa. In H. Lauer & K. Anyidoho (Eds.), *Reclaiming the human sciences and humanities through African perspectives* (Vol. 1). Accra: Sub-Saharan Publishers.

Fanon, F. (2008). *Black skin, white masks*. (Richard Philcox, Trans.). Berkeley, CA: Grove. (Original work published in 1952).

Ferguson, W. (2012). *419*. Toronto: Penguin Random House Canada.

Foucault, M. (1977). *Discipline and punish: The birth of the prison*. New York: Pantheon Books.

Frye, N. (2006). *Educated imagination and other writings on critical theory, 1933–1962*. University of Toronto Press.

Galeano, E. H. (1973). *Open veins of Latin America: Five centuries of the pillage of a continent*. New York: Monthly Review Press.

Gambos [Screen name]. (2007, September 2). Lady T—50th birthday party Video #1 [Video file]. Retrieved from https://www.youtube.com

Garuba, H. (1988). *Voices from the fringe: an ANA anthology of new Nigerian poetry*. Lagos: Malthouse Press.

Gates, H. L. (1999). *Wonders of the African world*. New York: Knopf.

Gilroy, P. (1993). *The black Atlantic: Modernity and double consciousness.* Cambridge, MA: Harvard University Press.

Gyekye, K. (2013). *Philosophy culture and vision: African perspectives.* Accra: Sub-Saharan Publishers.

Hopeless Africa. (2000, May 11). *The Economist.* Retrieved from http://www.economist.com

Hughes, L. (1921, June). The negro speaks of rivers. *Crisis.* Baltimore: National Association for the Advancement of Colored People (NAACP).

Ifedigbo, S. (2012). *The funeral did not end.* Lagos: Dada Books.

Irele, A. (1992). Dimensions of African discourse. *College Literature, 19*(3), 45.

Irele, A. (2001). *The African imagination: Literature in Africa & the black diaspora.* Oxford University Press.

Irele, A. (2011). *The negritude moment: Explorations in francophone African and Caribbean literature and thought.* Trenton, NJ: Africa World Press.

Irobi, E. Harlem. *African Writing,* 4. Retrieved from http://www.african-writing.com/four/esiabairobi.htm

Jameson, F. (1998). Postmodernism and consumer society. In *The cultural turn: Selected writings on the Postmodern, 1983–1998* (pp. 1–20). New York: Verso. (Original work published in 1983).

Jones, I., Thorpe, K., & Wootton, J. (Eds.). (2008). *Women and ordination in the Christian churches: International perspectives.* New York: Bloomsbury Publishing.

King Sunny Ade. (1979). Ariya is unlimited. *The royal sound* [LP]. Nigeria: African Songs.

Ki-Zerbo, J. (Ed.). (1981). *Methodology and African prehistory* (Vol. 1). UNESCO.

Kwei Armah, A. (1972). *Two thousand seasons.* Chicago: Third World.

Ladipo Manyika, S. (2008). *In dependence.* London: Legends.

Las Casas, Bartolomé de. (1992). *A short account of the destruction of the Indies* (N. Griffin, Trans.). London: Penguin. (Original work published 1552).

Lillehei, A. J. (2011, April). Limbé. In *Pigments in translation* (Honors thesis). Retrieved from https://wesscholar.wesleyan.edu/etd_hon_theses/706

Lotana O. (2008, April 24). Aso ebi. Urban Dictionary. Retrieved from http://www.urbandictionary.com

Maiwada, A. (2010). *Musdoki.* Abuja: Mazariyya Books, 2010.

Marvin, N. (Producer), & Darabont, F. (Director). (1994). "The Shawshank Redemption" [Motion picture]. United States of America: Castle Rock Entertainment.

Maryjince [Screen name]. (2007, August 12). Miss Feyi Balogun 25th birthday [Video file]. Retrieved from http://www.youtube.com

Matthews, H. L. (1940, February 7). France's struggle wins pope's praise. *New York Times.*

Retrieved from https://www.nytimes.com

Mbembe, A. (2001). African modes of self-writing. *Identity, culture and politics,* 2(1), 1–39.

Mbembé, J., & Rendall, S. (2002). African modes of self-writing. *Public culture,* 14(1), 239–273. doi:10.1215/08992363–14–1-239

McDill, Bob. (1978). Rake and ramblin' man [Recorded by Don Williams]. On *Country boy.* New York: ABC Records.

McKinsey Global Institute. (2010). Lions on the move: The progress and potential of African economies [Report]. Retrieved from http://www.mckinsey.com/global-themes/middle-east-and-africa/lions-on-the-move

Michaels, S. (2009, February 17). Michael Jackson's brother plans slavery theme park. *The Guardian.* Retrieved from https://www.theguardian.com

Moghalu, K. C. (2014). *Emerging Africa: How the global economy's "last frontier" can prosper and matter.* London: Penguin.

Mudimbe, V. Y. (1988). *The invention of Africa: Gnosis, philosophy, and the order of knowledge.* Bloomington: Indiana University Press.

Nduka, U. (1997). *Chiaroscuro.* Chicago: Yeti.

Nicol, A. (2011, August 18). The meaning of Africa. *African soulja: African poetry review.* Retrieved from https://afrilingual.wordpress.com/2011/08/18/the-meaning-of-africa-%E2%80%9-abioseh-nicol

Nkrumah, K. (1964). The African genius: Speech delivered at the opening of the Institute of African Studies on 25th October, 1963. Accra: Ministry of Information and Broadcasting.

Nnaemeka, O. (1995). Feminism, rebellious women, and cultural boundaries: Rereading Flora Nwapa and her compatriots. *Research in African Literatures,* 26(2), 80.

Nora, P. (1989). Between memory and history: Les lieux de mémoire. *Representations,* 26(1), 7–24. doi:10.2307/2928520

Nwaubani, T. (2009). *I do not come to you by chance.* New York: Hachette.

Obey, E. (2012). Oro mi ko lonso. *Ebenezer Obey in the 60's Vol. 1* [Digital download]. Ebenezer Obey Music Company.

Ofeimun, O. (1998). Postmodernism and the impossible death of the African author. *African Quarterly on the Arts,* 2, 24–47.

Oguibe, O. (2013). *I am bound to this land by blood: Collected poems.* Rockville, CT: Uhie.

Ogundipe-Leslie, M. (1994). *Re-creating ourselves: African women & critical transformations.* Trenton, NJ: Africa World Press.

Okigbo, C. (1964). *Limits.* Ibadan: Mbari Publications.

Okri, B. (2012, September 13). Full speech: Ben Okri honours Biko. *Cape Times.* Retrieved from http://www.iol.co.za/capetimes

Olukoshi, B. (2014, June 2). Random thoughts on African innovation [Keynote lecture delivered at the annual conference of the Academy of Sciences of South Africa (ASSAF), Pretoria].

Osofisan, F. (1996). Warriors of a failed utopia? West African writers since the 70s [lecture in Leeds University]. *African Studies Bulletin,* 61, 11–36.

Oyono, F. (1966). *Houseboy.* London: Heinemann.

Pagden, A. R. (Ed. & Trans.). (1971). *Hernán Cortés: Letters from Mexico.* New York: Grossman.

Palcy, E. (Director). (1983). *Sugar Cane Alley* [Motion picture]. France: Nouvelles Éditions de Films (NEF).

Paxton, T. (1967). Bottle of wine [Recorded by The Fireballs]. On *Bottle of wine.* [LP]. United States of America: Atco Records.

Perry, A. (2012, December 3). Africa rising. *Time.* Retrieved from http://time.com

Prakash, G. (1999). *Another reason: Science and the imagination of modern India.* Princeton, NJ: Princeton University Press.

Prince10008 [Screen name]. (2008, September 30). Yoruba night 2008 by United Yoruba International OKC pt 2 [Video file]. Retrieved from http://www.youtube.com

Renzetti, E. (2012, March 23). "'Allo, 'allo, what's all this then? Is it really going to cost more to get bladdered?." *The Globe and Mail.* Retrieved from http://www.theglobeandmail.com

Richburg, K. (1997). *Out of America: A black man confronts Africa.* Boston: Mariner.

Robinson, J. (2014, September 21). Watch Emma Watson deliver a game-changing speech on feminism for the U.N. *Vanity Fair.* Retrieved from http://www.vanityfair.com

Rodney, W. (1983). *How Europe underdeveloped Africa.* London: Bogle-L'Ouverture.

Rubadiri, D. (2004). Stanley meets Mutesa. In *An African thunderstorm and other poems* (pp. 24–26). Nairobi: East African Educational Publishers.

Senghor, L. S. (1948). *Anthologie de la nouvelle poésie nègre et malgache.* Paris: Puf.

Shoneyin, L. (2002). *So all the time I was sitting on an egg: Poems.* Ibadan: Ovalonion House.

Shoneyin, L. (2010). *The secret lives of Baba Segi's wives.* New York: William Morrow.

Simpson, S., Markgraaff, D. (Producers), & Hirsch, L. (Director). (2002). *Amandla!: A revolution in four-part harmony* [Motion picture]. South Africa/United Stated of America: Artisan Entertainment.

Soyinka, W. (1963). *Dance of the forests.* New York: Oxford University Press.

Soyinka, W. (1981). The critic and society: Barthes, Leftocracy, and other mythologies. *Black American Literature Forum,* 15(4), 133.

Soyinka, W. (2012). *Of Africa.* New Haven, CT: Yale University Press.

Thiong'o, N. W. (1986). *Decolonising the mind: The politics of language in African literature.* Portsmouth, NH: J. Currey.

Vargas Llosa, M. (1997). *Making waves: Essays.* London: Penguin.

Verdier, J. (1939). Introduction. *L'homme de couleur.* Paris: Plong.

Wainaina, B. (2006). *How to write about Africa.* Nairobi: Kwani Trust.

Walker, A. (2009). Jacksons star in Nigeria resort row. BBC News. Retrieved from http://news. bbc.co.uk

Watson, E. (2014, September20). Gender equality is your issue too [Speech transcription]. *United Nations Women.* Retrieved from http://www.unwomen.org

Williams, E. E. (1944). *Capitalism and slavery.* New York: Russell.

Wilson, A. (2003). *Gem of the ocean.* New York: Theatre Communications Group.

Wright, R. (1954). *Black Power.* New York: Harper Perennial.

Zac Brown Band. (2010). Colder Weather. On *You get what you give* [CD]. United States of America: Atlantic/Southern Ground.

Zeleza, P. T. (2003). *Manufacturing African studies and crises.* Dakar: Codesria.

Zeleza, P. T. (2014, October 13). Why I am afraid of the African disease of Ebola. In *Africa is a Country.* Retrieved from http://africasacountry.com

Index